AF754219

AROON TIKEKAR's interests go beyond purely literary scholarship. He developed early an interest in wider fields of enquiry like the history of modern Maharashtra. This is evident in his Ph.D. thesis, published in 1992 under title: 'The Kincaids: Two Generations of A British Family in the Indian Civil Service', and in 'The Cloister's Pale: A Biography of the University of Mumbai' (2006). The latter is an attempt to show how the city of Mumbai and its university, one of the oldest in India, grew almost together, culturally and intellectually. He was Editor of *Loksatta* between 1991 and 2002. He has delivered numerous memorial lectures. Presently, he is President of the Asiatic Society of Mumbai, a premier institution of higher learning in Western India, established in 1804.

Books by Aroon Tikekar

In English:

* The Kincaids—Two Generations of a British Family in the Indian Civil Service
* The Cloister's Pale—A Biography of the University of Bombay, 1984
* The Cloister's Pale—A Biography of the University of Mumbai, 2006
* Ranade—The Renaissance Man: What Has Happened to His Legacy?

In Marathi:

- Samaaj-spandane
- Jana-mana
- Taaratmya (5 vols.)
- Aswastha Maharashtra (2 vols.) (ed. by Vijay Tapas)
- Kaalmimaansaa
- Saaraansh
- Lele Ani Mee
- Ochyaa-Kochyaa
- Aksharnishthaanchi Maandiyaali
- Sthal-kaal
- Aisa Dnyaanasaagaru : Bakhar Mumbai Vidyapeethachi

Edited:

- Fast Forward—Speeches of Sharad Pawar on Socio-economic subjects
- Shahar Pune (2 vols.)

Translated:

- Bhaaratinchya Lalita Saahityakruti

Mumbai De-Intellectualised

Rise and Decline of a Culture of Thinking

Aroon Tikekar

"Wandering between two worlds, one dead,
The other powerless to be born..."

—Matthew Arnold, *Grande Chartreuse*

PROMILLA & CO., PUBLISHERS
in association with
BIBLIOPHILE SOUTH ASIA

NEW DELHI & CHICAGO

Published by
BIBLIOPHILE SOUTH ASIA
in association with
PROMILLA & CO., PUBLISHERS
URL : www.biblioasia.com

C-127, Sarvodaya Enclave
New Delhi 110 017, India

Copyright © Aroon Tikekar, 2009

First published 2009

All rights reserved

ISBN : 978-81-85002-97-2

Typeset in AGaramond
Layout and processing by Radius Arc, New Delhi

Printed and bound in India by
Bibliophile South Asia (Printing Division), New Delhi

This book is sold subject to the condition that it shall not, by way of trade or otherwise, be lent, resold, hired out, or otherwise circulated without the publisher's prior written consent; in any form of binding or cover other than that in which it is published and without a similar condition including this condition being imposed on the subsequent purchaser and without limiting the rights under copyright reserved above. No part of this publication may be reproduced, stored in or introduced into a retrieval system, or transmitted in any form or by any means (electronic, mechanical, photocopying, recording or otherwise), without the prior written permission of both the copyright owner and the publishers of this book.

To
My wife Maneesha

—the book emerged from
occasional discussions
with her

Contents

Preface

This small book is largely a compilation with necessary revision and enlargement of four lectures delivered by me between 1997 and 2007 on a theme of intellectualism in Bombay, or Mumbai as it is officially renamed since 1995. Although all the lectures appeared to have a sort of continuity in them, they were not exactly connected as they were written at different times. They were neither delivered chronologically, nor were the audiences same. Each lecture, moreover, was titled differently. Chronologically arranged their titles would have read as:

1. *An intellectual in today's society*, the 11th death anniversary of Madame Sophia Wadia Lecture, delivered on 26th April 1997 at the Theosophy Hall, Mumbai;
2. *The writer and society*, the 30th Lala Lajpatrai Memorial Lecture delivered on 28th January 2003 at the Lala Lajpatai College, Mumbai;
3. *Intellectualising of Bombay : formation of some early literary and scientific societies*, Special

Bicentennial Lecture, delivered on 25th April 2004 at the Asiatic Society of Mumbai; and

4. *The Minimum City: how and why Mumbai lost its intellectual leadership*, the Justice Mahadev Govind Ranade Oration, delivered on 13th March 2007, at the Convocation Hall, University of Mumbai.

It will be evident that the word Bombay or Mumbai, although used in the text for the city of Bombay or Mumbai in particular, applies on a general level to the entire area that was called the Bombay Presidency during the British rule, and which today constitutes the major area of the State of Maharashtra.

I had intended to present these lectures individually in thematic sequence rather than in the order they were delivered. However the gaps in the argument were wide and evident, and therefore required to be filled up. Some parts needed revision while a few ideas were found to be repetitive. I had therefore to rework on the texts of all the four lectures to bring cogency in the argument. The book did not consequently remain a collection of the 'four lectures'.

There are numerous books on modern Maharashtra that deal with one or many aspects of its history after 1818 when power was ceded to the British in this part of the country, yet there are not many that trace its intellectual history, with the exception of Rev. Matthew Lederle's *Philosophical Trends in Modern Maharashtra*

(1976). It will be presumptuous on my part to claim that this little book fills in the gap. I do not know whether it would be proper on my part to say that this book is a by-product of a larger book I am working on, which is: *Making of the Marathi Mind*, for I am not even sure whether I will be spared to complete a project as ambitious as this. This small book might, at best, offer readers some glimpses into the intellectual life in Maharashtra over the last one-and-a-half centuries. However that is not the real purpose behind this book.

For a concerned citizen of Mumbai today, it is painful to watch helplessly the withering away of the intellectual life, particularly within a few decades after gaining political independence. Mumbai in the pre-independence period had not only been the acknowledged commercial capital of India, but had also been providing intellectual leadership to other cities of India. Whether in social reform or in cultural renaissance, in literature or in theatre, in films or in sports, Mumbai had led the way. It had to its credit the sobriquet of 'the most progressive of the cities of India'. People from all corners of the country flocked to the city. Perhaps in the very success of Mumbai was the seed of its decadence. In barely four centuries of its known history, a sleepy village grew into a metropolis and started bursting at its seams due to overcrowding. A city which in the 19th century was well on the path of renaissance suddenly began showing signs of exhaustion and wearing out. Its composite culture was seen showing cracks on account of inadequate civic amenities and resultantly creating new social tensions. Mumbai today has lost its original lustre. Most citizens are looking to it as a place where material rewards come quickly. Any talk of culture in Mumbai has become almost puerile and impotent. The rabble has become the deciding factor. Politicians and the public both are watching the situation helplessly and ineffectually. The so called *vox populi* is in reality a cacophony of shrill voices of the opportunists interested only in their own welfare. Intellectuals belonging to liberal professions such as university or college teachers, editors of newspapers, writers and artists have already forsaken their social function and are happy to lead themselves lives of commoners. Is there any redemption for Mumbai from the cultural malaise or is a cultural demise the city's fate? Even an optimist will nurture in his heart a lurking feeling of doubt. It definitely must be disturbing to those who are concerned of its future. It is said that when culture declines, art flourishes. But those who could rebel silently through the fields of communication that they belong have already relinquished that responsibility. Mumbai today is in search of a saviour.

For me writing this book was a personal need and an individual catharsis. However, I should thank

Dr. R. Srinivasan and Professor J.V. Naik whose perceptive observations provided me various angles to analyse the malaise that Mumbai is struck with. S.R. Kasbekar who shares with me some of my interests and concerns was prompt in showing books he got before I could lay my hands on them. My wife Maneesha was a great advantage when around, for getting a nod from her, difficult as it is, gave me strength. Author and critic Raji Narasimhan's comment that this book needed to be written as the frustrations of being an Indian today in India are not confined to poverty and material want and that she woke it anew after reading the script, encouraged me more. She did not stop at reading the script, but went through it carefully and suggested improvements without changing my arguments.The librarians at the Rajabai Tower University Library, particularly Tilaka Joseph, Varsha Deodhar, Neeta Kulkarni, Alka Patankar, attended to an impatient reader's demand for books, as promptly as they could. I am thankful to all of them. Last but not the least, I must thank my friend Ashok Butani who was after me to complete the book right from the moment I discussed the idea with him.

—Aroon Tikekar

1

Who is An Intellectual?

Nirad C. Chaudhuri, in the Preface to his monograph, *The Intellectual in India* (1967) had said: "All over India those who have any intellectual ambitions and aptitutes are discouraged. Authoritarianism in politics and social life which runs deep among the Hindus, hostilities or apathy to intellectual activities, to precarious economic situation of the intellectual who has most often to sell himself to make a livelihood—have all tended to make him feel frustrated if not wholly paralysed." Four decades have passed since these words were written and the situation in India appears to have worsened. It is true that such a situation cannot continue indefinitely for all times to come and the downward curve has to rise at some point of time. Many competent minds have discussed the aetiology of the disease of de-intellectualising and presented the diagnosis of the malady of cultural slidedown; some have even suggested prescriptions for recovery, but to no avail. The gravity of the situation is hardly seen causing presently even a ripple in society.

Mumbai* was during the pre-independence days leading the entire Presidency and also the nation in the intellectual field. Then how did it lose its position of leadership? What have been the reasons for its losing that position? After the flourish that the city witnessed in the 1960s and part of the 1970s, the city has suffered a cultural retreat. Mumbai's intellectual decline has affected other cities in Maharashtra and they too have developed a dislike towards anything that has a stamp of intellectual activity. Respect for scholarship has become a thing of the past. Unlimited hypocrisy pervades all the liberal professions. Is there any relationship between cultural slidedown and intellectual detestation? Obviously, there is. Let us begin with some discussion on what intellectualism means.

There are obviously no definite prescriptions for the intellectualisation of society. In the absence of a precise definition of intellectualisation only descriptive indications can be recorded.

The concept of intellectualisation surely refers to the process of inculcating, assimilating and adhering to reason, rationality and progressive ideas including

---

* Since most of the societies mentioned in this discussion, established and flourished as they were in the 19th century, incorporate the word 'Bombay' in their name, Bombay is used throughout to avoid frequent oscillation between Mumbai and Bombay. Similarly readers are requested to note terms such as the Bombay Presidency, the Bombay Province and Mumbai, the State capital of Maharashtra.

scientific development which endeavours to unravel the secrets of Nature. For any intellectualised, or for that matter intellectualising, society such varied and enriched social and cultural activity is an essential condition. This, in other words, means not only giving preference to societal intellectual achievement over just individual intellectual attainment, but also denotes an acceptance and admittance of plurality of ideas. Intellectualising a society further means willing participation in various debates and discussions in an attempt to assess and evaluate the veracity and efficacy of traditionally held opinions and beliefs about the physical sciences that aim at unravelling the secrets of Nature and also investigating and experiencing the mysteries of the metaphysical world. This still further means the evaluation and revaluation of a living tradition. Intellectualising a society also means the acceptance of a belief that social change is both desirable and is possible through human endeavour. Intellectualising the society means increasing socio-cultural and political awareness by creating a public space for everyone in the society with a view to making him or her ultimately a responsible and concerned citizen. This awareness in the end results in creating and strengthening a civil society through previously established associations and organisations, and also establishing new ones to suit the contemporary world, thus, leading the community into becoming a civil society with a civic culture. A civil society with a civic culture generally results in the blossoming of public life in all its aspects. A pre-requisite for such a blossoming of a society is obviously that it becomes 'a knowledge society' in essence, for knowledge empowers people, and lack of it impoverishes. As proper knowledge is derived from pure reason, it enables individuals to think, to analyse, and to understand the situation around in a proper perspective.

Mumbai, for instance, presents a unique case. The city was seen in the 19th century as being well set on an enlightened path. It provided intellectual leadership to the entire country. But somewhere on the way it lost its initial advantage. Now it is showing signs of being in a de-intellectualised state in almost all walks of life, despite its commercial success. Why this should happen to the most progressive and industrialised city in India, needs an investigation. An attempt is made in this small book to spot the lacunae in the psyche of the people living in Mumbai, the shortcomings of the local institutions, and also the manner in which the Western elements were imbibed due to the British and the European contact that influenced the local traditions and produced generation that was once described as the one that was torn between two civilizations. "...the two-fold life—the divided and conflicting life that we have to live in the midst of two civilisations..." remarked Justice Mahadeo Govind Ranade at a public meeting condoling Justice Telang's premature death (*Life and Work of late Mr. Justice M.G. Ranade*, 1902, vol. I, p. 107). Some discussion on intellectuals and their social responsibility is initiated here. This is followed by an analysis of the present "intellectuals" in four fields, viz. the academia, the media, literature and culture, for it is the failure of these four liberal professions to deliver that has by and large brought the society to a de-intellectualised condition. Of course, throughout the discussion there are references to contemporary politics, as an undercurrent which affects all the four fields.

★★★

The year 1862 was a milestone in the intellectual history of the city of Bombay. In the first ever Convocational Address of the University of Bombay as it was then called, four Arts Faculty students and four medical students were awarded graduation degrees and certificates. In his Address, Chancellor Sir Bartle Frere had called upon them to disprove the belief that the Oriental intellect was worn out and that it was no longer capable of producing results which could only ensue from a higher order of intellect. The premier graduates took up the gauntlet and started the process of the rejuvenation of their society that was suffering from 'a paralysis of thought' (so described Ranade, the 'prince among graduates', the condition of the society around him). With the loss of intellectual vigour came the eclipse of its pristine cultural glory. The restoration of a society plagued by disorder and intellectual stagnation is the work for at least a century. But these premier graduates saw a dream in the words of Sir Bartle and they set themselves immediately to work and contributed their mite. The history of Maharashtra in the late 19th century tells us that the generations that followed the premier graduates, reached nearest to the point of realisation of that dream. Then something went wrong and society started backsliding on the path of progress. The year 1862, therefore, marks a watershed in the intellectual history of modern Maharashtra and with it begins another phase of the intellectualising of Bombay. But before duscussing the rise and decline of intellectual in Bombay, it is necessary to explain who is an intellectual and what is meant by intellectualising a society.

★★★

The concept of the intellectual is a historical category. It emerged in the modern world when certain objective and subjective conditions matured. Even then, the term has defied precise definition and means different things to different people. Reference to the term also evokes different responses in different societies and also from generation to generation, depending on the socio-cultural milieu. While in all societies it evokes a feeling of respect, at times it also becomes a pejorative term implying social derision.

The word 'intellectual' used as a noun emerged largely in the 19th century Europe; first in the 1860's, to designate that section of the university-educated youth who were 'critically thinking personalities' as described by Pisarev or by 'nihilists' as referred to by Turgenev. University education instilled in them a spirit of inquiry which questioned the traditional value system by applying to it the criteria of reason and social comfort. In his *Communist Manifesto* Karl Marx described intellectuals as a group of bourgeoisie who took upon themselves the task of uplifting the working classes and shaping their ideas of a classless society. The term 'intellectual', thus, was initially associated with the ideological Left, but in the 20th century it has come to be used rather differently; it came to include *inter alia* the 'culture bearers' of society as also the 'upholders of traditional values'. (*The Fontana Dictionary of Modern Thought*, 1977, p. 428) Only recently has it acquired a more comprehensive meaning and includes all those who endeavoured to promote and defend all humanist values. This is a remarkable change in the meaning of the term. All definitions however seem to be unanimous in that the intellectual is one who swims against the current of popular passions and politics of the day, thus remaining detached from the society around him. And that makes him different from the fellow members of the society.

Although the term intellectual as used today is of recent origin, the social necessity and functions of a class of intellectuals are described by social philosophers from Plato to John Stuart Mill, from Manu to the founders of the Servants of India Society. Plato's concept of a philosopher-king is no different from the functions of the intellectual class in a present-day democracy. Plato was aware of the fact that the "common people generally disapprove of philosophers". He also knew that "individuals who mix with the crowd and want to be popular with it, will always dislike a philosopher." Yet he felt that 'a philosopher-king' was a possibility. What is the necessity of a philosopher, one may ask. To which Plato has given an apt answer. He has even distinguished a teacher from a philosopher. He says, "All those individuals who make their living by teaching, and whom the public call 'sophists' and envy for their skill, in fact teach nothing but the conventional views held by the mass of people; and this they call science." To differentiate philosophy from science, Plato has taken the example of a large and powerful animal. He says:

> "Suppose a man who is in charge of a large and powerful animal, and made a study of its moods and wants; he would learn when to approach and handle it; when and why it was especially savage or gentle; what the different noises it made meant, and what tone of voice to use to soothe or annoy it. All this, he might learn by long experience and familiarity, and then call it science, and reduce it to a system and set up to teach it. But he would not

> really know, which of the creature's tastes and desires was fair or unfair, good or bad, right or wrong... But is there any difference between him and the man who thinks that the knowledge of the passions and pleasures of the mass of the common people is a science, whether he be a painter, musician or politician?" (*The Republic*, Book VI).

The philosopher follows his conscience, takes the side of truth and defends it at all cost, fights for social justice, opposes any encroachment on or curtailment of freedom and, to use an oft repeated expression, upholds humanism. This is not possible unless one has a clear insight into the past and a vision of the future. If he does not understand the history which has fragmented the reality and if he cannot fathom the future in the light of the fragmented reality, he cannot be a thinker or a philosopher: "No one can be a great thinker who does not recognise that as a thinker it is his first duty to follow his intellect to whatever conclusions it may lead," said John Stuart Mill, "Truth gains more even by the errors of one who, with due study and preparation, thinks for himself, than by the true opinions of those who only hold them because they do not suffer themselves to think." (*On Liberty*, 1859, p. 62) Thinkers in any society are required to maintain the freedom of thinking. "Not that it is solely, or chiefly; to form great thinkers that freedom of thinking is required." According to Mill, "On the contrary, it is as much and even more indispensable, to enable average human beings to attain the mental stature which they are capable of. There have been, and may again be, great individual thinkers, in a general atmosphere of mental slavery. But there never has been, nor ever will be, in that atmosphere an intellectually active people" (*On Liberty*, 1859, p.62). In such a period of time, we cannot hope to find that generally high scale of mental activity which has made some periods of history so remarkable.

Of what use is a philosopher, a thinker, or an intellectual to society? What social function does he have in a democratic set-up today? Does he have a social function? With his disinterestedness in the day to day affairs of society, and with his well-groomed power to think about its welfare, he assumes the role of a custodian of the tradition of creative and critical thinking. It must be explained at the outset that I do not wish to use the word 'intellectual' in the sense it is commonly used. On a more serious level the collective noun 'intellectuals' stands for those 'culture bearers', or 'culture leaders', whose social function is to propound theories and create concepts to be then applied to the behavioural pattern of a society. I intend using the word to refer to those who are convinced that there is no power greater than the power of ideas. Therefore, they like to translate many of their ideas into creating institutions for reforming and thus in the ultimate analysis, intellectualising, the society around them, be they social thinkers or preachers, University teachers or writers, newspaper editors or jurists.

Scepticism is the root of all progress. Are the custodians of the tradition of creative and critical thinking really necessary for the society? If so, then why? John Morley delineated the role of 'the thinking people', when he said:

> "Progress depends upon tendencies and forces. But these tendencies and forces, the organs and representatives must plainly be found among the men and women of the community, and cannot possibly be found anywhere else. Progress is not automatic, in the sense that if we were all to be cast into a deep slumber for the space of a generation, we should awake to find ourselves in the greatly improved social state. The world only grows better; even in the moderate degree in which it does grow better; because people wish that it should, and take the right steps to make it better: Evolution is not a force, but a process; not a cause, but a law." (*On Compromise*, 1921, 1933 ed.; pp. 126-27).

It is the intellectuals who direct the society on the road to progress. This is their principal social function. A society whose intellectuals shy away from their responsibility is sure to go into a deep slumber. Material progress without proper ideological grounding or commitment can spell deterioration and imbalance. Gramsci is more precise in defining the role of intellectuals in society. According to him even if all men are potentially intellectuals in the sense of having intellect, not all are intellectuals by social function. Gramsci divides intellectuals into two groups. There are, according to him, 'traditional' (professional) intellectuals, legal, literary, technical, etc. and there are the 'organic' intellectuals. The 'organic' intellectuals, according to Gramsci, are defined by their role in production, as well as in the organisation of work. Their competence gives them a leading position and they therefore can also perform the political role of directing or forming opinion for the workers. For my purpose here, I would like to restrict my observations only to the 'traditional' intellectuals, since this is the main focus of this book. Therefore, I feel more at ease with the nomenclature given to these two groups by Edward Said, who in his *Reith Lectures* (1993) called the 'traditional' intellectuals as 'amateur' intellectuals as against the 'professionals', performing the social obligation of intellectuals.

For Edward Said, an 'amateur' intellectual himself, intellectuals are individuals with a vocation, that of representing, whether by talking, writing, teaching, or appearing on television. He prefers to call 'amateur' intellectuals 'vocationals' rather than 'professionals', and feels that the intellectual ... is neither a pacifier nor a consensus-builder; but someone whose whole being is staked on a critical sense, a sense of unwillingness to accept easy formulas, or ready-made cliches, or thc smooth, cvcr-so-accommodating confirmations of what the powerful or conventional have to say, and what they do. Not just passively unwilling, but actively willing to say so in public.

Said perhaps uses the word 'amateur' as an antonym of 'professional'. This is clear when he emphasises that the intellectual can perform his social function effectively only if he is universal in his orientations rather than specific. Only by virtue of his being universal and a dispassionate outsider can the intellectual develop a critical sense about everything around him. "The intellectual today", says he, "ought to be an amateur, someone who considers that to be a thinking and concerned member of a society one is entitled to raise moral issues at the heart of even the most technical and professional activity as it involves one's country, its power, its mode of interacting with its citizens as well as with other societies."(*Representations*, 1994, p. 61) To do this every intellectual must have his audience and a constituency. A teacher or a university professor has a class full of future citizens, a writer has his readers, an editor has thousands of readers of his newspaper, a telecaster has thousands and thousands of viewers, a trade union leader has his expansive electorate of union members.

Said, thus, appears to be in agreement with Gramsci on the role of the intellectual in society. The intellectual is surely distinguishable from 'a faceless professional' or a competent member of other classes. The intellectual, unlike the professional, represents a view-point, an attitude or a philosophy or an opinion. He does not hesitate to raise disturbing questions to confront orthodoxy and dogma or regressive and corrupt practices of persons who hold positions of power, thereby making the rest of the members of society think and rethink about their actions. To do this, the intellectual has to be a dispassionate outsider. Only by virtue of being universal in approach and detached in attitude can the intellectual develop a critical sense about everything around him.

In every industrial society today, the class of intellectuals has become a distinct social class. The expansion of higher education and the growing concern for cultural development have contributed to the importance and growth of this class, which enjoys a certain status in society. A person who expresses concern about socio-cultural problems and contributes to the 'thinking' of the society may be regarded as a custodian as well as an enricher of the cultural tradition. As a teacher or a university professor, an artiste or a journalist, or a cultural commissar, if he promotes his ideas of the normative problems of the society, he could well be termed an intellectual. There are otherwise no fixed yardsticks to identify the intellectual in society. An intellectual identifies himself or is identified by the social group he belongs to. This is, of course, an informal arrangement.

The intellectual traditions of the West significantly differed from those in India. In the West, no doubt, there was a tremendous spirit of enquiry, cutting down the fetters of intellectual slavery, accompanied by a revolutionary urge towards a better future which made Renaissance possible. The Renaissance men with their non-conformism often literally stood on the edge of the precipice, willing to take the risk of being called heretics, fearlessly spoke the language of Truth as they saw it and appealed to reason rather than sentiment or tradition. Such a phenomenon never became a part of Indian history. Not that we lacked basic humanistic thoughts. There are numerous, although stray, references to universal humanism in devotional literature which, for example, is epitomised in the *Pasaaydaan* of the *Dnyaaneshwari.* But the fact is that these thoughts which remained in the realms of spiritual imagination and wishful thinking did not prompt the rulers of the day to translate them into social reality. Hinduism was primarily concerned with individual salvation on the basis of transcendental values and obsessed with life after death, although there is a substantive life-affirming trend in Hindu thought. It is a moot point if the Brahminical scriptures ever had consideration for the entire society and its welfare. There are, of course, references to '*naagarak*' (ancient version of today's *naagarik*, meaning 'citizen'), in Vatsyayana's *Kaamasutra* (in a Section of the book called, *Naagarakavruttam*) suggesting that there was a consideration of the social life of people (Chakladar, 1954, p. 103). Buddhism which tried to seek an answer to this problem and stood for *samata* and *karuna*, was born here, but flourished elsewhere till Dr. B.R. Ambedkar revived it and gave his own interpretation of *Dhamma*. The fact is that Ambedkar chose Buddhism because it is the only atheist religion in the world. It revolves round secular ethics and not god. But the irony of time is that his followers made a God out of him.

It is true that a series of invasions resulting in loss of political freedom, held a real or imaginary threat to the social system. This in turn, however, created an urge to retain culture with its pristine form thereby making the people inward looking and defensive of all tradition. Any suggestion or recommendation for change became blasphemy or sacrilege. In short, our society withdrew into its shell. The resultant orthodoxy and obscurantism rang the death knell to intellectual growth. If things had been otherwise, many social and ethical aberrations in our society would have disappeared in the normal course of its evolution. It is a fact that our hide-bound and more or less stagnant society, whose intellectuals were more concerned with life after death with an almost total recourse to fatalism, began to loosen up only under the forces that came in the wake of British rule.

2

Intellectualisation of Bombay

Let us now try to apply these yardsticks and preconditions of change to the city of Mumbai. This city, as is known, was essentially a British creation. From the moment the British set their eyes on this naturally protected harbour, they decided to develop it as a trade-centre in the East. In fact there is room to believe that they wanted the city of Bombay to develop as the London of the East, just as the Portuguese tried to develop Goa as "Tropic Rome". Bombay did develop in the 19th century as the *Urbs Prima in Indis,* the premier city in India. It did not remain merely an emporium of the East and a trading centre for long; it in no time became the commercial capital of the country. Editor Robert Knight, who was prompt in noticing the quick financial growth of the city, changed in 1861 the title of his newspaper from the *Bombay Times* to *The Times of India* and, announcing the change, he remarked in the very first editorial that the city had already become 'the commercial capital of India'. (*The Times of India*, 28 Sept. 1861) Bombay then was witnessing an expansion all round. Ever since it became the seat of power after the fall of the Peshwas of Poona in the early decades of the 19th century, 1818 to be exact, it had been confronted with regular influxes of people from far off places. The city and its seven islands developed at a speed without parallel in Indian history. A sleepy hamlet within a short span of a few centuries emerged into a busy international commercial town where fortunes were made and lost overnight. With the new thrust given to formal Western education people of all religious faiths and communities flocked to Bombay in search of education and employment. Schools and colleges came to be established. A University was granted for Bombay alongwith those at Calcutta and Madras by the Charter of Queen Victoria in the same year of assuming Imperial power following the rebellion all over India. Although some of the teachers might have taught with the intention of proselytising under the pretext of schooling and teaching them, Bombay was fortunate to have at the helm of affairs some of the most competent and visionary administrators like Mountstuart Elphinstone, Sir John Malcolm and a little later Sir Bartle Frere. Did they not know what effect the Western education would have on local youth? They did. Mountstuart Elphinstone wrote to his friend in so many words: "It may be urged that, if we raise the natives to an equality with ourselves by education and at the same time admit them to a share in their own government, it is not likely they will be content with the position assigned to them, or will ever rest until they have made good their title to the whole." (Cotton, 1892, p. 189)

Apart from the governmental policy framers, Bombay was fortunate in having highly meritorious teachers whose contributions to the city will be ignored only by the ungrateful. If one goes through their memoirs and those of their illustrious students, one gets a peep into the academic atmosphere in the 19th century Bombay. Sir Alexander Grant and Professor William Wordsworth are only two of the outstanding names. It is recorded that Professor Grant used to take with him students of his such as Ranade, Pherozeshah Mehta and K.T. Telang for long evening walks and discuss with them various topics under the sun. Professor Grant later became Vice-Chancellor not only of the University of Bombay, but later of the Edinburgh University too. He took many popular as well as unpopular decisions as Vice-Chancellor in Bombay. It goes to the credit of Professor Grant for introducing to the students here Western concepts such as liberalism, rationalism and humanism. One has to browse through the archives of the University of Bombay to see how some of the British professors fought to keep the autonomy of the premier educational institution in western India intact.

Then there were the British jurists who contributed significantly to the development of the social psyche of the people. Were their judgements always just, one may ask. But one can at the least surmise that they were by and large fair. Justice Joseph Arnould's judgement in the Maharaj Libel case (1861)—"What is morally wrong cannot be theologically correct"—must have given tremendous strength to the social reformers of the times.

University educated youth must have been inspired by the intellectual outputs of newspaper editors such as Dr. George Buist, Robert Knight and Mathius Mull. Multifarious contributions of Dr. George Birdwood to the city were a class apart. One can write a tome on British and European contributions, particularly of the Scottish and Irish residing in Bombay at one point of time or another in the 19th century. To put all the British and the European savants in one basket branding them as "imperialists" without analysing their individual contribution to Bombay's development will be unfair, to say the least.

If Bombay quickly came to the forefront of socio-cultural life in the Deccan and the Konkan, it is, at least initially, to a significant extent due to the contributions of these teachers, jurists and journalists. In addition to the ever increasing number of schools and colleges, many institutions of higher learning came to be established, taking inspiration from those started by the British. Newspapers in regional languages were being published in the city. The names of early newspapers such as *Darpan* (Mirror), *Dnyaanodaya* (Rise of knowledge), *Dnyaan-prakash* (Light of knowledge), and *Digdarshan* (Direction of progress) were enough to proclaim their objective and intent—for spread of knowledge coming from any world, Western or Eastern, was their prime objective. Bombay has never looked back commercially since those times. It continued to lead in commerce, trade, banking and industry. Its commercial success also paved the way for its socio-cultural progress, and in due course, more importantly, it came to epitomise a national conscience in matters of social as well as cultural importance, thanks to the enlightened British men of vision steeped in the liberal tradition of Europe who headed various fields of social activity—educational, journalistic or judiciary. They not only promoted education among local inhabitants, but also encouraged social and cultural change. Under their guidance, Bombay learnt lessons early in multi-religious, multi-cultural cohabitation. With the cosmopolitan social fabric of the city, the inhabitants of Bombay acquired from the beginning the sobriquet 'India in miniature'. These were surely signs of blossoming.

At the beginning of the 19th century, the nascent modern city of Bombay was waking to a new sensibility due to contacts with Europe and especially, Britain. New aspirations of a cosmopolitan Bombay were in the air. The city was soon to experience the formation of literary and scientific societies, initially a novelty but later a proud achievement, which aimed at the diffusion of knowledge. To those deeply rooted in the oriental tradition of individual intellectual attainment, the corporate intellectual activities of these literary and scientific societies were perhaps a new experience. With every new institution of higher learning formed and nurtured by the European—chiefly British—men of calibre, fresh from witnessing the changes brought by the Reformation and the Renaissance in their countries, who were otherwise ordained to perform a special duty in an alien land, a fresh opportunity was gained by Indians to observe the working of corporate intellectual activities, initially from a distance and later, when membership of these 'Societies' was thrown open to them, from actual participation in their proceedings. The experience of corporate intellectual activity was enriching, to say the least. It surely was the beginning of the process of intellectualising Bombay, for which eminent historian V.K. Rajwade had used a more appropriate word—*mandalikaran.* By the middle of the 19th century, Bombay became a beehive of literary and scientific societies: Students Literary and Scientific Society (est. 1848), Marathi Dnyan Prasarak Sabha, Gujarati Dnyan Prasarak Sabha, Juvenile Society of Science and Literature (est. 1854), the 'Satya Vichar Sansud', the Native Book Club and many other such societies that aimed at the intellectual development of individuals. Many of these were surely direct imitations of the early societies in Bombay, viz. the Literary Society of Bombay (est. 1804), the Agri-Horticultural Society of Western India (est. 1830), the Bombay Geographical Society (est. 1835), the Bombay Medical and Physical Society (est. 1835) and some others. The intellectual proceedings of these societies, indeed, had a cascading effect on the emerging new elite who were introduced to Western ways and views of life, the life of the English in particular.

The diffusion of knowledge being the sole objective of these early societies, they were different from the later associations. The attempts of corporate activities, chief among them being the Paramhansa Sabha (est. 1847), the earliest anti-caste movement, the Bombay Association (est. 1857), the first political organisation, and the Prarthana Samaj (est. 1867), the Bombay Presidency Association (est. 1885) that really paved the way for the Indian National Congress that was founded in Bombay in the same year (1885), were all oriented towards socio-religious and political reform. And as such they were headed by people who were intellectuals by temperament and reformists by inclination. This is the second phase of intellectualising of Bombay that ultimately brought in a kind of renaissance in Western India. If the former societies aimed at intellectualising its members, the latter ones intended to instil in their members the reformist zeal. That the later varieties sprung from the earlier ones cannot however be denied. In the first phase of the Indian societies, or, to use the contemporary term, 'native societies', socio-religious and political reforms were kept outside the purview of their spheres of activity. For instance, the Students' Literary and Scientific Society stayed clear of religious and political issues (Masselos, 1974, p. 29). The spirit of socio-religious reform and political activism was understandably the advent of later years. The early literary and scientific societies in Bombay were solely directed towards the intellectual advancement of their members, reading papers, discussing them, debating over the data collected, supplementing the known facts and thus adding to one's knowledge, developing one's own intellectual acumen. It is often forgotten that the early literary and scientific societies served as launching pads for the subsequent intellectual development that ultimately showed the path of progress towards renaissance of Western India.

The Literary Society of Bombay was the earliest society established in 1804 for the diffusion of knowledge. It was the first of its kind in the whole of Western India and was the oldest society of learning, second only to the Bengal Asiatic Society founded by Sir William Jones and Warren Hastings in 1783 in Calcutta (R.P. Karkaria, *The Athenaeum,* December 24, 1904, p. 875). Both have continued to exist. The moving spirit behind the Literary Society of Bombay was Sir James Mackintosh (1765–1832) who had come to Bombay in February 1804 as Recorder of the Supreme Court of Bombay (today's Chief Justice of the Bombay Hight Court). Sir James who had studied medicine at Edinburgh was known to have spent most of his time in pursuing his interests in politics, literature and society, even at the cost of his medical profession. He ultimately acquired legal training and was called to the Bar from Lincoln's Inn in 1795. India always attracted him and he had intended to come here as Advocate-General, a position that he was denied till the end. But before he came to Bombay, he had resolved "to do all in his power to promote the progress of knowledge within the future sphere of his influence; and among other means of effecting the purpose of investigating the philosophy, sciences, arts, literature, geography, and history of India". (Tivarekar, 1886, p. 8)

On landing in Bombay, he found the city a cultural wasteland. There was little intellectual activity that would interest him. He started looking around for men of high literary interests and, within a year announced the establishment of the Literary Society of Bombay. The high-flown ideas with which he inaugurated the Literary Society on 26th November 1804, may even today be the ideals for any such society. "The smallest society" he had said, "brought together by love of knowledge is respectable in the eye of reason; and the feeble efforts of infant literature in barren and inhospitable regions are in some respects more interesting than the most elaborate works and the most successful exertions of the human mind. They prove the diffusion at least, if not the advancement of science; and they afford some sanction to the hope that knowledge is destined one day to visit the whole earth, and in her beneficent progress illuminate and humanise the whole race of man." *(Transactions,* 1819; 1877 reprint; vol. 1, p. xiii). The words of Sir James just fall short of naming two modern concepts—'civil society' and 'knowledge society', but precisely sum up both the concepts.

It is the establishment of the Literary Society of Bombay that marked the beginning of the process of intellectualising the city of Bombay.

That the establishment of The Bombay Literary Society would meet with the express approval of the government of the time was obvious. For, among those who attended the preliminary meeting of the Literary Society of Bombay held at Parel House (today's Haffkine Institute) were Jonathan Duncan, Governor of Bombay; Sir James Mackintosh himself who was Recorder of Bombay; Stuart Moncrieff Threipland, Advocate-general; Dr. Helenus Scott, First Member of the Medical Board; William Dowdswell, Barrister-at-Law; and Lieutenant-Colonel Brooks who later became Military Accountant General at Bombay.

Some of those who attended the preliminary meeting like Charles Forbes and Robert Drummond were to distinguish themselves soon by their contributions to the history of the city of Bombay. In the same meeting Sir James Mackintosh was elected President, Charles Forbes Treasurer and William Erskine Secretary. Paucity of funds was even then the main hurdle. With the permission of the governor in Council, therefore, the hurdle was overcome by raising money by a lottery.

Like any other society, the Literary Society of Bombay too suffered problems in its infancy. For, though it began well by fulfilling its foremost object which was the foundation of a public library, concluded on 25th February 1805, a bargain for the purchase of an expensive library, built by various people of the medical establishment in Bombay for over half a century. The society, however, found it difficult to pursue its next project mooted by the President himself. He wanted the members to collect materials for a statistical account of Bombay. He had specially prepared a set of "*Queries the answers to which would be contributions towards a statistical account of Bombay*" and had offered to supervise the project. The project could never really take off. Sir James' *Queries* are published as Appendix A of the Vol. 1 of *Transactions* and are a model for any preliminary sociological survey of a new area. In 1806, he, with the approval of the members of the Literary Society, forwarded a proposition to the Royal Asiatic

Society to create a fund in England that could be used towards publishing and translating Sanskrit works. Though the plan for the creation of a special fund did not materialise, it was decided to publish translations from time to time.

For nearly 35 years the activities of the Literary Society and the Bombay Branch of the Royal Asiatic Society as it came to be called since 1830, were out of bounds for Indians. The Indian educated elite were deprived of the knowledge of the proceedings of the Society's 'academic' meetings, as they were neither allowed to be its members nor was there any journal that could have informed them of its activities.

The objects for which the Literary Society was founded were the promotion of literary and scientific investigations more immediately connected with India, and the study of the literature, the antiquities, the arts and the sciences of the East generally. Reading and discussions on papers by its members, and the establishment of a comprehensive library were the means adopted for achieving the objectives. (Tivarekar, 1886, p. 7)

The Literary Society of Bombay grew from strength to strength as its efforts for the diffusion of knowledge were appreciated, and those of scholarly temperament found the platform provided by the Society extremely useful. Lieut-Colonel Joseph Boden, who later became the founder of the Boden Professorship of Sanskrit at

Oxford; Captain John Briggs who not only collated and edited Ferishta's history but also translated *An Autobiographical Memoir of the early life of Nana Farnaves* and wrote the well-known work—*The cities of Gujarashtra;* Robert Drummond who published the earliest grammar of the Marathi and Gujarati languages; William Erskine who wrote *Life of Babur and Humayun* in two volumes, and translated the Memoir of the Emperor Babur; Captain Basil Hall, known for his many books describing his extensive travels; General Vans Kennedy whose works on the Hindu mythology and the origin and affinity of languages have been given the status of Indian classics; major Edward Moor, the author of the *Hindu Pantheon* and *Oriental Fragments;* Captain W.H. Sykes who compiled *Land Tenures of the Deccan* and wrote *'Notes on the Religious, Moral and Political State of Ancient India'* and contributed numerous papers to the Journals of various societies; these and many others were the members of the Literary Society of Bombay, and "lent their names to the Society to build its reputation as the foremost Literary and Scientific Society in Western India". *(Mandlik,* Preface, 1877)

Commensurate with the objectives of the Society, it was necessary to have a well-stocked library. It became more and more difficult to acquire books with the initial subscription of Rs. 60 per annum. The subscription was raised to Rs. 100 per annum in

1811. It became, therefore, necessary to increase the number of readers of the library and consequently increase the usefulness of the library to the public at large. Thus were admitted persons who were not members of the society as subscribers at the same rate of subscription as the regular members, that is, Rs. 100 p.a. It created two classes of members—(a) members who were either resident or non-resident; and (b) subscribers. This arrangement remained in force till 1874, when the category of life-members was introduced for the first time. Besides the paying members, the Society had provided for the election of honorary members. The honour could be conferred on distinguished foreigners or any other persons who have "materially contributed to promote the objects of the institutions, either by donation or otherwise". (Tivarekar, 1886, p.11-12)

Initially the Literary Society of Bombay being open only to Europeans, it was out of bounds for the local people. It did not matter much in the early decades of its existence. But as more and more young Indians started taking to Western education—with the American Marathi Mission starting the Hindu Boys School in 1815, the Native Education Society's School established in 1824, Dr. John Wilson starting his Free General Assembly Institution School in 1832, later developing into the Wilson College, and the Robert Money High School established in 1837, and also with the Elphinstone Institution started in 1822, later blossoming into a College bearing the same name in 1835, and in the case of the city of Poona the Poona Sanskrit College came to be established even earlier in 1821—local pupils developed a desire to seek light coming from any quarter, East or West. Although some sane voices from both communities having greater social interaction in all community endeavours pleaded induction of local youth as members, it took a long time for Indians to get admitted to the Literary Society of Bombay—or the Bombay Branch of the Asiatic Society of Great Britain and Ireland as it was later called. Sir John Malcolm, for instance, was one of the earliest to see the impropriety of keeping Indians away from corporate intellectual activity. When voted President of the Society, he made a pointed reference to it. While eulogising Mountstuart Elphinstone for his extraordinarily sympathetic attitude to the Indian community and for providing an efficient and enlightened administration for over seven years, Sir John said on 5th December 1827:

> "Our interest and reputation will hereafter be greatly promoted by the gradual diffusion of science and useful knowledge through the means of the institutions that have been recently founded for the instruction of the natives in this quarter of India. The attainments these must acquire in such seminaries cannot but lead to that happy association

> between them and their European fellow subjects, which will essentially aid and facilitate the future labours and researches of the Literary Society of Bombay." (Tivarekar, 1886, p. 12)

Maneckji Cursetji was the first Indian who sought to be a member of the society. He was initially proposed in 1833 by Robert C. Money, Persian secretary to the Government of Bombay. The President, Colonel Vans Kennedy, also supported his candidature. In fact, he proposed that "all natives entitled to sit on grand juries should be eligible to (the membership of) the Literary Society," a proposition which was objected to by the Rev. Dr. John Wilson on the ground that it would give preference over their countrymen of the highest literary attainments to those whose only literary qualification was acquaintance with the English language. Therefore, the doors of the Society were not opened for Maneckji Cursetji in particular and for Indians in general. Maneckji, however, was not disheartened; he continued to knock at its doors. After over two decades of the useful existence of the Literary Society of Bombay came a proposal from the Royal Asiatic Society of Great Britain and Ireland for a union between the two institutions. The proposal was considered in the Literary Society's specially convened meeting on 5th December 1828 in which Sir John Malcolm reviewed the work done by the Society in Bombay. A special committee was appointed to consider the merger, which gave its report on 3rd January 1829 and within a year the Literary Society became an integral part of the Royal Asiatic Society, London. Soon after the amalgamation of the Bombay Literary Society, with the Royal Asiatic Society of Great Britain and Ireland, the Town Hall was also completed in 1831, where the B.B.R.A.S. as it was known for over a century, shifted its office and activities. With the merger of the two institutions Maneckji Cursetji who was already elected a member of the Royal Asiatic Society of Great Britain and Ireland, had to be given membership of the B.B.R.A.S. The doors of the Society were thus ultimately opened to Indians on 29th January 1840. He was soon followed by Jagannath Shankershet and Sir Jamshetji Jejeebhoy and many others. Obviously, by 1886, nearly one third of the Society's members were Indians.

Over the years the B.B.R.A.S. attained considerable prestige and distinction. Among its distinguished honorary members were Sir Gardiner Wilkinson, Professor Monier Williams, Dr. A. Weber and among notable contributors, Dr. Murray Mitchell on Marathi Poetry, Dr. Carter upon Oriental Literature, General Jacob on translations of inscriptions, Sir Bartle Frere on descriptions of cave temples, Justice Newton on ancient coins of Western India, Dr. Bhau Daji on inscriptions, coins and Sanskrit literature (his enviable manuscript collection adorns the cupboards of the Society even today), V. N. Mandlik on Sanskrit inscriptions,

Dr. George Birdwood upon Indian economic history and commercial geography, and Dr. R.G. Bhandarkar. Dr. George Buhler, K.T. Telang, Dr. George Buist, Professor A. Orlebar, Dr. Gerson Da Cunha, Edward Rehatsek, Dr. Lisboa... the list of eminent scholars and researchers can be extended. However it is not the purpose here to narrate the history of the Literary Society of Bombay or its later *avatar*, the Bombay Branch of the Asiatic Society of Great Britain and Ireland.

The reputation of the Society was built not only on the quality of the researches conducted there but also on the collection of books which increased with every new donation in cash or kind, be it from Jagannath Shankarsheth, or from Cowasji Jehanghier, or Premchand Roychand or Dr. Bhau Daji, or Malcolmson. The Bombay Literary Society, which transformed itself in 1830 into the B.B.R.A.S. was the embodiment of the corporate intellectual life of the Bombay city. Soon after the establishment of the University of Bombay, in 1857, its graduates did their university proud by their intellectual attainments through the B.B.R.A.S. in diffusing the knowledge they had painstakingly earned. William Frere, President of the B.B.R.A.S. in 1864, described the situation in these apt words:

> "The Society is now, I must say, on the verge of a revolution... I cannot contemplate the vast increase

in the number of Europeans I now see in Bombay, nor the high standards of education required by the University, without feeling confident that there must be many among the Europeans who have pursuits higher and more learned than that of mere money-getting; and that there must be recruits for our Society among them; and I will not believe that a hundred men can graduate at the University without ten of them at least becoming not only members, but working members of the Society. We shall then, I trust, find the notes of the Parent Society verified and that our branch, though never severed from the Parent Stalk, may still itself claim to be a tree." (Tivarekar, 1886, p. 50)

The seed of corporate intellectual activity in Bombay sowed by Sir James Mackintosh had not only germinated but also was about to flower. The flowerings of that seed were varied. Intellectualism grew in almost every field. The establishment of the Agri-Horticultural Society of Western India in 1830 was only one of them. Its chief promoter was Sir Sidney Beckwith, then Commander-in-chief and Acting Governor of the Bombay Presidency. The society's only objective was to encourage agriculture and horticulture in Western India in a more scientific manner. Its expenditure was met by subscriptions, public donations and grants from government. The first President of the Agri-horticultural Society was Mr. Newham and the first Secretaries Mr. Vanfill and Sir Jamshetji Jejeebhoy.

In 1835, the Society acquired land at Sewri, which was laid out as a garden by Colonel Dickinson and Fr. Heddle, assisted by an expert European gardener. More land was granted to it in 1837 and again in 1840. Under the meticulous supervision of the gardener and Fr. Giraud and Dr. George Buist, it did not take much time for it to earn the distinction of being a well laid botanical garden, the first of its kind in western India. Dr. Buist, an exceptionally talented Scotsman who had come to Bombay in May 1840 as editor of the *Bombay Times,* carried out the general arrangement of the land, while Dr. Giraud and later Sir George Birdwood (1832–1917) paid more attention to the botanical sections of the garden. The Sewri botanical garden was maintained until 1862, when its plants were transferred to the Victoria Gardens (today's Jijamata Udyan). The Victoria Gardens also were looked after by the Agri-horticultural Society until 1873, when the society ceased to exist. With the plants transferred to Byculla and the Society outgrowing its public utility, the 52,000 square yard Sewri (today's Shivadi) garden was turned into a cemetery for Europeans of the Protestant, Roman Catholic and Scotch Presbyterian churches (*The Gazetteer of the Bombay City and Island,* Vol. 3, 1909, p. 65).

The Agri-Horticultural Society of Western India showed tremendous vitality between the years 1840 to 1865 and cultivated among the citizens of Bombay a new awareness about gardening. Sir George Birdwood who was the first curator of the Victoria and Albert Museum, has made the citizens of Bombay indebted for life from his numerous contributions to the civic and intellectual life of the city in the previous century. One of earliest contributions to the city by Sir George was converting into a garden and pleasure-ground 33 acres of low-lying and barren land which were named Victoria Museum and Albert Museum, now renamed Dr. Bhau Daji Museum and Byculla Zoo, now renamed Jijamata Udyan. The credit for highlighting the need to cultivate a scientific approach goes to the Agri-horticulture Society, which carried on its useful work for over three decades. However, when one remembers the after-effects of the Share Mania that afflicted the city during the early 1860s, one sadly realises why the good and intellectualising work carried out silently by various societies came to an abrupt halt. Societies like the Agri-Horticultural Society fell victim to the climate of general bankruptcy in the city. The city, which was taking some good lessons in philanthropy, received rude shocks that almost undid the earlier good work.

Like the Literary Society of Bombay, the Bombay Geographical Society too played a major role in the intellectualisation of Bombay in the early 19th century. This Society was established at the instance of Mountstuart Elphinstone. While leaving Bombay after retirement, he must have left his heart behind. As its objective, the Society put before it encouragement of geographical researches in Western Asia and the neighbouring counties. Lord Clare and Sir Charles Malcolm took a lead in its establishment. From the very start, the Bombay Geographical Society looked for advice to the Royal Geographical Society of London. It eventually became a Bombay Branch of the Royal Geographical Society.

J. F. Heddle, who later became the first Secretary of the Society, was a keen geography enthusiast. In a letter addressed to the Secretary of the London Society, he once said:

> "Bombay enjoys several facilities which if properly and judiciously directed may lead to important and valuable results. From the extensiveness of the Hon'ble East India Company's Dominions, European officers, both Military and Civil, are found distributed over a vast tract of (the) country, and possess full opportunities of acquiring a perfect local knowledge of their respective districts either by personal observation or through the medium of natives whose language they generally understand. On the other hand the Hon'ble Company's ships of war are always cruising in the Arabian and Persian Gulf and in the Indian Ocean, and Naval gentlemen in command of them have already rendered important services to geography by their surveys and charts and are capable of accomplishing much more in that way" (quoted in the *Magazine*

of the Bombay Geographical Association, 1953; Vol. I, No. 1, pp. 10-11).

The first meeting of the Bombay Geographical Society was held in the rooms of the B.B.R.A.S. on 9th April of that year in which Governor the Earl of Clare, Sir J.W. Awdry, W. Newham, James Farish, Major-General J.S. Barnes, Lieut-Colonel Vans Kennedy, Lieut-Colonel E. Hardy, Lieut-Colonel D. Barr, Major J.G. Griffiths, Captain J. Griffiths, B. Northon, George Adam, J. Sutherland, J. Wedderburn, Rev John Wilson, Rev J. Lawrie and many others were present. (*Bombay Courier*, April 2, 1831) Many of these names are to be found in the history books as of those who led the Society in various aspects of intellectual life in the city. R.C. Money acted as the officiating Secretary till Heddle could be duly elected. Captain Sir Charles Malcolm was elected President. Immediately after its formation, the Bombay Geographical Society issued a circular to all its members about the objectives of the Society. The circular impressed upon its members the importance of the study of geography in all its aspects. It encouraged the members by emphasising the fact that whereas it was difficult to make any addition to the existing knowledge about European geography in India and around, it was rewarding to explore and study territory which was almost virgin.

From 1832 to 1836 the Bombay Geographical Society did not publish its proceedings separately.

They were included in the proceedings of the Royal Geographical Society of London, which also published all important papers read in the Bombay Branch. In *Transactions* of 1836, for instance, is published an interesting paper by Lieut. Alexander Burns (who later went to Kabul as the British envoy and was unfortunately assassinated) on the maritime communications of India as carried on by the 'natives' particularly from the Cutch area. Lieut. Burns had maintained in the paper that it was the natives of India, and not the Arabs, who conducted the trade between India and Egypt, a claim that is challenged in the same journal by Lieut. Dickinson. Such exchange of views and evidence was sure to benefit the Society at large as it brought historical truths to the fore by clearing cobwebs of history. That, surely, a corporate form of intellectual activity.

From 1837 onwards the Bombay Geographical Society began to publish on its own its proceedings in Bombay. It felt the need to lead an existence independent of the London Society. A reply by the Secretary of the Royal Geographical Society, London, to the Secretary of the Bombay Geographical Society was a tribute to the excellent work done by the Bombay geographers:

> " ... I am desired to offer our sincere congratulations on your having come to the determination to stand alone and on having already given such good proof of your ability to do

so and we fully agree with the opinion expressed by the Governor-in-Council that, 'an infinitely stronger stimulus to exertion is thereby applied to members of the Society in India, than if the memoirs etc. were only to be published in Europe'. Your proceedings already show the wisdom of the advice, and it will be more evident as your publications become more widely circulated, and so, far from the change affecting any previously existing relations between the Society's (except in the name) it does but strengthen the great bond which should unite us all, viz. the determination to diffuse all the information we are able (to gather) and to labour for the advancement of geographical science and discovery." (quoted in the *Magazine*, of the Bombay Geographical Association, 1953, Vol. I, No. 1, p. 13)

There are in all 19 volumes of Transactions of the Bombay Geographical Society beginning with 1837, and the last published in 1873, the year when the Bombay Geographical Society was merged with the B.B.R.A.S. Dr. Heddle, the first Secretary of the Bombay Geographical Society who continued to hold the position till 1842, put the Society on an academically sound foundation and handed over his responsibility to Dr. George Buist who had become a member immediately on coming to the city to take charge as editor of the *Bombay Times.* To Dr. Buist—a man of natural gifts, tremendous energy and exceptional talents—Bombay owes a lot. During the next 16 years of his tenure as Secretary of the Bombay Geographical Society, he made it a beehive of activity. He himself contributed well-researched papers on subjects such as hurricanes, hailstorms, meteors, volcanoes, which are even today considered pioneering contributions in their respective fields. These contributions earned for the Society international repute. The fame of *Transactions* spread in Europe as well as in America.

One of Dr. Buist's regular and valued contributions to geographical studies of his time was an annual survey of geographical researches carried on during the year. He also made a catalogue of the most remarkable hailstorms which occurred in India between 1822 and 1860. It was at Dr. Buist's instance that meteorological and tidal observations began to be recorded in Bombay, Karachi, Aden and other places. In fact, he is said to have initiated the study of the science of meteorology in India. He himself was in charge of the Colaba Observatory between 1842 and 1844. While still holding charge in May 1844, he conducted for the officers of the Navy, a course of lectures on natural philosophy, chemistry and natural history, which was also open to the public free of cost. (The *Bombay Times,* August 9, 1845)

Dr. Buist was in those days a moving spirit behind most scientific societies in Bombay. During one of his visits to England, he was requested to collect geological specimens for the Museum of Elphinstone College, which he did painstakingly. He also conducted a series of experiments on the clays and argillaceous earth found in and around Bombay, with a view to improving the conditions of pottery manufacturers. Dr. Buist is also credited with introducing the art of glazing and woodcut engraving in Bombay, having for a long time cut with his own hands the blocks used in the issues of the *Bombay Times.* Few men, who devoted themselves to literary and scientific avocations, have surely employed their time to more fruitful advantage than Dr. Buist.

Dr. Buist's career in Bombay between 1840 and 1857 displayed the spirit of Messianism, albeit self-proclaimed, that he had inculcated when he was ordained by the Scottish Church before coming to Bombay. However, his life reveals contradictions in character, which ultimately ruined his reputation built over twenty years. Due to his unscrupulous anti-Indian views during the 1857 revolt by the Indians, he had not only to lose the editorship of the *Bombay Times,* but also face ignominy. The citizens of Bombay despised him everafter when they discovered in him a strong subterranean and perfidious sense of British superiority. It is one of the many ironies of the history of 19th century Bombay that a man of such rare natural abilities who, after having accomplished so much, who would have retired from the country of his adoption with glory and respect from the people for whom he sowed the seeds of public development, who worked assiduously for the welfare of under-privileged sections of the society, who even spent all his earnings at the risk of emptying his coffers, in reality accomplished so little, not enough even to keep his memory green. (Tikekar, 1988, p. 98)

Dr. Buist's self-proclaimed Messianism initially included encouraging educated Indians to form societies of learning such as the Bombay Geographical Society and the Asiatic Society and thus participate in corporate intellectual activities. His encouragement to Dr. Bhau Daji (1824–1874) and Naoroji Furdoonji (1817–1885) and the entire group of Elphinstonians which for their reformist zeal came to be known as the 'Young Bombay Party' is recorded in the pages of the *Bombay Times* of the period. These very Indians went against him, when he, as if lost balance, started calling Indians 'ferocious tigers', 'fit only to live in caves', and successfully sought to remove him from the editorial chair.

Till 1843 Indians were not admitted to the membership of the Bombay Geographical Society, just as in the B.B.R.A.S. In the year 1843-44 appears among its members for the first time the name of the distinguished Indian, Balshastri Jambhekar (1810–1846) to whom is rightly accorded the singular honour of being 'the pioneer of Renaissance in Western India' and also as 'the Founder of Modern Maharashtra'.

Although Balshastri was admitted to the membership of the Bombay Geographical Society as late as in 1843, a few of the papers that he had submitted to it, were read at its meetings and were, apparently, appreciated. From Balshastri's time the Society's records show the names of more Indians. Ali Mahomed Khan was elected a member in 1845. He was followed by Maneckji Nusserwanji, Dhanjibhoy Framji and Vinayakrao Jagannath in the same year. In as late as 1850, one comes across the name of Jagannath Shankershet himself, and in 1852, Dr. Bhau Daji and Dr. Narayan Daji, the two illustrious brothers were admitted. By 1864-65, the number of Indian members of the Bombay Geographical Society went up to 42. It is recorded that though the Indians did not initially seem to have taken part in the proceedings by way of reading papers or delivering lectures, they helped the Society in other ways. They were regular in attendance and also gave substantial donations. In the report of the Bombay Geogrphical Society for the year 1864-65, the President W.E. Frere records:

> "To the native gentlemen we are indebted for allowing the Society to partake of that unprecedented wealth which Bombay now enjoys. Mr. Cursetjee Furdoonjee gave us Rs. 1500. Mr. Premchund Roychund Rs. 5000, Mr. Sorabji Pestonji Framji Rs. 1000, and today we have received Rs. 3500 from Mr. Bhagwandas Purushottamdas." (*Transactions*, 1868, vol. 18, p. ix)

Philanthropy in the cause of socio-cultural and intellectual activity was surely a part of the process of intellectualisation. No systematic study of social philanthropy of the wealthy and elite class in 19th century Bombay exists as it does about New York city. In her book *Why the Wealthy Give: The Culture of Elite Philanthropy*, Francie Ostrower traces, through numerous interviews of the concerned, the elite philanthropy, "an institution [that] ...plays a central and defining role in upper-class culture." (*Why the Wealthy Give?,* 1995, Introduction). Among many reasons of social philanthropy such as religion, ethnicity and gender, the chief one has always been "giving back to society..." For the inner urge of the wealthy to give back to society a share in their bounty may be at time of retirement from business, on the occasion of the death of a near and dear one, or for improvement of one's own community in a renascent society has, no doubt, roots in the growing intellectualism. For the 19th century Bombay there was yet another aspect of social philanthropy. Social philanthropy was an act of either a mistrust of the alien governmental power and large scale bureaucracy or it was respecting the wishes of the alien statesmen desirous of improvement in the local people. However, it was no doubt, a social habit to donate for the public cause. Seeking 'legitimacy' for the wealth acquired was a later phenomenon.

But to revert to the Bombay Geographical Society, Dr. Buist was replaced as Secretary to the Society by

D.J. Kennelly. By 1865, however, amalgamation of the Bombay Geographical Society with B.B.R.A.S. was mooted. Sir George Birdwood observed that such a step would be advantageous to both the Societies. He said, "it would be difficult for the Geographical Society to hold its own, now that the Indian Navy had been done away with, whereas by joining the Asiatic Society it would become a favoured partner in an income of Rs. 30,000 a year. By the amalgamation, the monthly meeting of the United Societies would be more interesting and their common volume of transactions more valuable." *(Magazine,* 1953, pp 13-14)

Though the talk of amalgamation started in 1865, the actual merger took place only in 1873. The property of the society worth Rs. 22,440, along with the Government grant of Rs. 50, the Premchund Roychund Fund amounting to over Rs. 2,000 and the Bhagawandas Purushottam Fund amounting to about Rs. 500 were handed over to B.B.R.A.S. The contribution of the Bombay Geographical Society towards the intellectualisation of 19th century Bombay compares with that of the Literary Society of Bombay, which transformed itself as the B.B.R.A.S. However, as far as scientific advancement is concerned, the Bombay Geographical Society had no parallel in the first half of the 19th century. With accounts of the first marine surveys, especially those of Bombay and Madras, detailed accounts of the Great Trigonometrical

Survey of India, elaborate accounts of Land Tenures of Konkan, detailed reports on the Indian Ocean islands, and many other well-researched papers based on actual investigation, *Transactions* have continued to be tremendous source material for geographers and geologists. Even research papers on Africa and Persia and the neighbouring countries of India have been pioneering contributions by those who have become venerable names in these fields today.

Apart from the significant findings of Dr. Buist, noteworthy and pioneering contributions of R.X. Murphy *(Remarks on the History of Some of the Oldest Races Now Settled in Bombay,* Vol. 1, p. 128); D. J. Kennelly *(Earthquake of the 29th of April 1864 in the North-Western part of the Bombay Presidency,* Vol. XVII, p. 288); Capt. James MacMurdo *(Observations on the Indus or Sindhu River,* Vol. Ill, p. 124); James Burgess *(Remarks on the Bombay Tidal Observations for 1861*, XVII, p. 1); Capt. G. Wingate *(Remarks on the Laterite of the Southern Conkan and Southern Marhatta Country,* vol. X, p. 287) need be mentioned. Even Sir Bartle Frere when he was Commissioner in Sind wrote in *Transactions* an article on 'Heavy Rain in Scinde in July and August 1851 and its effects on Cultivation'.

The Mechanics Institute was another Society, which catered to the intellectual needs of Bombay at one time. Established in 1847 for the mechanics of the Bombay Mint and the Dockyard with Chief Justice Sir

Erskine Perry as its President, it aimed at maintaining the latest literature on mechanics and also arranging for lectures on literary and scientific subjects. Its meetings were initially held in the premises of the Dockyard. However, after the demise of Sir Robert Oliver in 1848 it was moved to a rented place in the Fort area, but ultimately the Town Hall became its venue. Dr. John Wilson, for instance, lectured on 'The Wandering Classes and Tribes of Western India' on 16th January 1865 and on 'The Marhatta Country and Its Tribes and Castes' (*The Times of India*, 17th March 1869). He developed these lectures later in his book on Indian castes. The details of the lectures organised at the Mechanics Institute are difficult to obtain. However, some of the lectures, published as separate booklets show that renowned professors like Sir Alexander Grant lectured there off and on. In one of his lectures at the Mechanics Institute titled 'Rome, England and India', delivered on 7th January 1863, Sir Alexander made a prophecy about the future of India, which makes interesting reading today. He said:

> "India is not ripe for parliaments and it is beginning to grow too advanced for durbars. If a private individual might be allowed to venture a prophecy in such a matter (that is, enlargement of constitutional liberty), it would be that the durbar character of these councils will diminish and the representative or parliamentary element increase; and that these bodies will gradually be more and

> more entirely trusted with the management of local affairs, with which they must be far better acquainted than any central authority, however wise, could be."

Sir Alexander cogently argued and concluded his argument by saying: "After all it is perhaps the highest art and the highest possible achievement to put people in a position to manage their own affairs." It is encounters with such spirits of enquiry and liberal ideas that instilled in the minds and hearts of the then newly educated elite thoughts about their country's future.

An example to remember is that of Sir Alexander Grant, who wielded significant influence on his students during the decade he was in the city. As Principal of the College, Director of Public Instruction and also as Vice-Chancellor of the University of Bombay, he was a force to reckon with. It was he who persuaded donors such as Cowasji Jehanghier and Premchund Roychund to donate huge amounts for public causes including buildings for the University. He grew friendly with Bartle Frere, Governor and Chancellor of the newly formed University and the duo did miraculous work in Bombay as far as the University was concerned. More importantly, Sir Alexander showed that he could take unpopular decisions in the interest of students. It was he who, as Vice-Chancellor, took a bold decision of discontinuing the teaching and studying of 'vernacular' languages such as Marathi, Gujarati, Canerese as Kannada was then called, and Hindustani languages barely within three years after the University started awarding degrees, on the ground that the literatures in them, apart from that of the saint-poets, 'lacked maturity' and 'variety'. However unpalatable the decision was, it was not totally untrue and therefore had to be accepted by those concerned. Such an evaluation of the local literature by a foreigner prompted people of the stature of Ranade and others who started Granthottejak Sabha, a society for the promotion of books; Granthkaaraanche Sammelan, a conference of authors; Vaktrutvottejak Sabha, a society for the promotion of public speaking; in addition to establishing public libraries in as many cities of the Bombay Presidency as possible. It took efforts spanning nearly four decades to start the study and teaching of 'vernacular' literatures in the University. Sir Alexander Grant, was truly a moulder of opinion.

3

Mumbai's Intellectual Leadership

In the year 1863, the Mechanics Institute became a beneficiary of David Sassoon's largesse. With the assistance of the Bombay government, which not only gave land, but also an additional grant to complete the building of its own. In its new *avatar*, the David Sassoon Library from 1870 onwards became a focal point of the library movement in Bombay. Many public libraries which were started around the middle of the 19th century drew their inspiration from the Bombay Literary Society Library, the Bombay Geographical Society Library and the Sassoon Mechanics Institute Library, notable among which were Framji Cowasji Institute and its Library with its Free Reading Room facility (started in 1845), the Juvenile Improvement Library (started in 1852), the library of the Petit Institute, which initially began as Philosophic Institute in 1855 and, the Gujarati Sabha, which was started in 1865. The last one later assumed the name of

Alexander Forbes (1821-1865). The Forbes Gujarati Sabha did commendable work in Bombay for over a century as far as the advancement of learning was concerned, as among its objectives were the collection of Gujarati manuscripts, translation and publication of works from other Indian and European languages and awarding prizes to writers and researchers.

Dr. Bhau Daji who was one of the earliest of the generation of beneficiaries of European awakening in Bombay, took the lead in all attempts at the intellectual awakening of the local people. In a meeting organised at the Sir Jamshetji Jejeebhoy Parsi Benevolent Institution on 13th January 1855, he not only summed up the situation, but also gave his futuristic projection. "I have felt," he once said, "that there is too much ground for the reproach that has been cast upon our educated young men, that after leaving their Alma Mater they cease to procure that intellectual nourishment which a cultivated and growing mind requires. I am convinced that the time has come when a well-supplied News-room and Reading Room must be provided; that the effects of such a source of information will soon be visible in the increased intelligence of the community; and that proof of intelligence and spirit thus afforded by the Natives will not be without its effects on the European mind." (*The Bombay Telegraph and Courier*, 16th January 1855; quoted in Priyolkar, 1971, p. 178)

When a medical college was established in Bombay, it was proper that it was named after Sir Robert Grant, for as Governor it was he who had really promoted the spread of medical education and the idea of founding a medical college in Bombay also was mooted by him. But he did not live to see his dream fulfilled due to his abrupt and untimely death at a comparatively young age. Following the establishment of a medical college it was also natural that a medical society was mooted. And so eventually the Grant College Medical Society came into existence in 1852. But before more reference is made to this society, it must be mentioned that the very first such society in Bombay set up in 1789 was curiously called the Medical and Literary Society, established by persons belonging to the medical profession. The excellent book collection of this Society later formed the nucleus of the Literary Society of Bombay. Another attempt of medical men to form a Society was in 1835. This time they called it the Medical and Physical Society. This Society too does not seem to have really taken off. It also was ultimately merged with the B.B.R.A.S. However, the third attempt in November 1851 was successful, perhaps due to the infrastructure available at the Grant Medical College. Dr. Peit, who was selected to preside over the Society's proceedings, had the support of Dr. Coles, Dr. Bhau Daji, both as Vice-Presidents, and Dr. Carvalho as Secretary.

The papers on medical subjects that were read in

the meetings of the Grant College Medical Society are mentioned in the Annual Reports of the College. More significant for my observations is the object with which the Society was started. Dr. Morehead, the Principal of the Grant Medical College has stated: "The importance of contributing means of encouraging in the young medical men of India those habits of continued systematic study and accurate observation, without which there can be no successful cultivation of medical science or useful practice of medical art, was felt by my colleagues equally as by myself. We knew that in European countries the institution of Societies had done much towards developing and maintaining a spirit of scientific co-operation and of friendly professional intercourse." (*Annual Report 1851-52*, 1852, p. xix) It was to achieve similar results that the Grant College Medical Society was started. It will be unfair to say that it did not achieve much of the objective for which it was launched.

However, the direct and almost immediate impact of these and other literary and scientific societies started by Europeans with the sole purpose of the diffusion of knowledge was seen in the establishment of the Students' Literary and Scientific Society in 1848, by a group of young Elphinstonians which later came to be called the 'Young Bombay Party'. The members of the 'Young Bombay Party' were never a closely-knit group like the 'Young Bengal' under the tutelage of Henry Derozio (1809–1831). 'The Young Bengal' was a group dissimilar to Young Bombay in almost every aspect of dissent with the old order. However, fired by an ardent desire to bring in reform in every walk of life they came together initially to usher in rays of enlightenment in the society around them. Although in the early stages the Students' Literary and Scientific Society functioned under the guidance of the English Professors Paton, Henry Green, L.R. Reid and Dr. John Harkness (retired as Principal of Elphinstone College in April 1862 after a service of more than twenty-five years), its protagonists were the young students who had finished their schooling at the Elphinstone Institution and Naoroji Furdoonji —'Naoroji Master'—was undoubtedly their leader. Naoroji Furdoonji taught at the Institution between 1839 and 1845 and was then appointed Interpreter at the Supreme Court of Bombay. Himself a student of Balshastri Jambhekar, the first Assistant Professor at the Institution, Furdoonji also had the privilege of being Balshastri's colleague as the second Indian Assistant Professor. At a time when Balshastri was excelling in all benevolent and intellectual enterprises in Bombay this 'very first flower on the shrub of English education' (Tikekar: *The Cloister's Pale,* 1984, p.13) was plucked abruptly. After Balshastri's untimely death in 1846, at the age of 36, the mantle of leadership fell on Naoroji Furdoonji. If Balshastri started a newspaper called *Durpan,* Naoroji started his called *Vidyasagar,* both with the sole object of diffusion of knowledge among their countrymen.

The Students' Literary and Scientific Society was the first major step for the Young Bombay Party. Along with their educational activities they also started the Marathi Dnyanprasarak Sabha and Gujarati Dnyanprasarak Sabha. Regular meetings of these two sabhas were conducted where papers on serious literary and scientific subjects were read. Among the members of the Students' Literary and Scientific Society were men of the calibre of Dadoba Pandurang (Tarkhadkar), Ram Balkrishna (Jaykar), Dr. Bhau Daji (Lad), Sorabjee Shapurjee Bengalee, Dr. Atmaram Pandurang (Tarkhadkar), Bhogilal Pranvallabhdas, Bhaskar Pandurang (Tarkhadkar) and many others. These names are written in bold letters in the history of the latter half of 19th century Maharashtra. Their lives and works helped the Society to go nearer the realisation of the dream unveiled to them by Sir Bartle Frere. That the dream was not destined to be fully realised is another matter. The Students' Literary and Scientific Society proved to be the cradle for all socio-religious and political reforms in the 19th century. And the formation of such a parent society was possible only because of the literary and scientific societies established earlier by well-meaning Europeans.

The general spread of Western education resulted in accelerating the process of the intellectualisation of

Bombay, and forming literary and scientific societies became the order of the day in the city. But discussions across the table began centering round socio-religious reforms followed soon by political agenda rendering the original objective of spreading knowledge confining to the back rooms. Two cultures, which were coming nearer to each other in the process, suddenly faced an atmosphere of mutual suspicion after the 1857 rebellion. Literary and scientific societies began to be replaced by various caste and community organisations and single-objective associations. It was but natural. The Bombay Association mooted in 1851, Bombay Branch of East India Association in 1867 and the Bombay Presidency Association in 1885 and others of the ilk gained preference over the express objectives of the earlier societies formed for the diffusion of knowledge. It will be appropriate to say that the various socio-religious reforms, some successful, others not quite, by the Associations and the achievements of Indian National Congress which had its very first session in Bombay in 1885, were the outcomes, directly or indirectly, of the work done by the early literary and scientific societies.

The formation of societies, however, was not totally abandoned. Attempts were made also to revive defunct societies. The Bombay Photographic Society established in 1856 with Dr. G.R. Ballingal as President, H.D. Cartright as Vice-President and

W.H.S. Crawford as Hon. Secretary, had two Indians —Dr. Bhau Daji and his brother Dr. Narayan Daji— among its founder members. It had fallen on bad days in the period of financial gloom, but was again revived. The Natural History Society, started in 1856, and promoted by Dr. Don, Dr. Leith, Dr. Carter and Dr. Buist had proved short-lived. Another attempt in 1885 with a similar objective "of exchanging notes and observations on zoology, and of exhibiting interesting specimens of Indian life" by eight residents of Bombay under a similar name, the Bombay Natural History Society, established in 1885, was so successful that it ultimately blossomed into a world known organisation and, in due course, celebrated its centenary. Among its eight founder members, two were Indians. These eight persons were J. MacDonald, E.H. Aitkin (more known by his initials EHA), Colonel Swinhoe, J.C. Anderson, J. Johnstone, Dr. Atmaram Pandurang (Tarkhadkar), Dr. Maconochie and Dr. Sakharam Arjun (Raut). The Anthropological Society of Bombay whose honoured members were Sir Monier Williams, Professor T.H. Huxley, Professor Montegazza, Professor J. Damesteter, and Dr. Adolf Bastian, was formed in April 1886 under the Presidentship of Edward T. Leith, and had as its objective: "the prosecution of anthropological research in India, by investigating and recording facts relating to physical, intellectual and moral development of man, and more specially of the various races inhabiting the

Indian Empire." This society too ultimately merged with the B.B.R.A.S. Mention must also be made of the Bombay Art Society which was founded in 1888 for "encouraging art particularly among amateurs, and educating the native public to an appreciation of its merits."

A brief survey of the 19th century literary and scientific societies is attempted here only to show how social interaction among intellectuals, both Europeans and Indians, was a great asset in intellectualising Bombay Society in its early phase. I wish to reiterate that the process of intellectualising the city of Bombay was started by the British intellectuals. Intellectual curiosity about the land of their adoption, its people and their living tradition definitely did prompt them to collect information and produce knowledge. Their initial interaction with the local residents, however restricted, did not meet with any resentment or resistance. The literary and scientific societies therefore flourished and remained productive for a few decades. But with the study of the English language and introduction to European literature and Western thought in general through higher education and with educated Indians being allowed to enrol as members of the various societies of learning it became more and more obvious that although both were for some time going together hand in hand, their ways were bound to diverge. Mountstuart Elphinstone's prognostication was sure to come true. He had written to his friend,

James Mackintosh, the inspiration behind the Literary Society of Bombay, that "...the belief that our Indian Empire will not be long-lived is reason and not prejudice. It is difficult to guess the death it may die... The most desirable death for us to die of should be, the improvement of the natives, reaching such a pitch as would render it impossible for a foreign nation to retain the government... A time of separation must come; and it is for our interest to have an early separation from a civilized people..." (Cotton 1892, pp.185-86).

Educated Indians, or the new class of intellectuals were more and more convinced that whatever the Western scholars were doing, it was, in the ultimate analysis, to help strengthen British rule in the land. The world was soon to witness the high noon of imperialism and with the Indian realisation of the imperialist designs the worlds of both were never the same again. Societies prosecuting socio-cultural research languished giving way to socio-political associations. Yet it cannot be denied that the scholar volunteers of the early decades contributed significantly to the spread of both scientific and liberal ideas that shaped the coming generations of educated Indians. The pioneering work of these early literary and scientific societies spread new awareness about society and history, social reform and faith in human endeavour, in addition to scientific knowledge.

It is only after the establishment of the three universities in India in 1857, that a new intellectual class began to emerge, a class that began to question the irrationalities that had crept into the traditional value system. So it was with Western India. Four distinct types of Indian intellectuals emerged during this period. The first type led by Balshastri Jambhekar, that wanted reform to come from within and on evolutionary lines, conforming as far as possible, to the Hindu *shastras* and tradition. Jambhekar was our very first social reformer during the British rule. He was the founder of an intellectual tradition that inspired people like Mahadev Govind Ranade, Ramkrishna Gopal Bhandarkar, Kashinath Trimbak Telang, Vishwanath Narayan Mandlik and Bal Gangadhar Tilak, a tradition that eagerly accepted the 'light' coming from the West and was eagerly ready to dissociate itself from the ills of its own religious and cultural tradition. Each of these reformers, of course, was different from others including their predecessors, and made an advance over his predecessors. For instance, Ranade and Bhandarkar chose the socio-religious field, while Tilak and Mandlik opted for the socio-political field. Their commonality in thinking was that they wanted to build the new India on old foundation. The second type was represented by Vishnu Bhikaji Gokhale, better known as Vishnubava Brahmachari, who wanted to reject anything and everything Western and base social progress only on the ancient Vedic Dharma. This class was of those who could be called revivalists. The third type was represented by Gopal Ganesh Agarkar that did not wish to have any revivalist props, but based its ideas of social good and progress in the light of the new knowledge gained from Western thought and marshalled the old texts in support of social reform on reason and conscience. Agarkar and his followers disdained the strategy of relying on tradition. For them any debate propped on authority, traditional or modern, temporal or spiritual, was bound to be sterile. In this respect they were closer to Max Weber who spoke of legal rational authority. There was yet another type of intellectual who emerged from the masses. That was Jotiba Phule. He was undoubtedly the first and the best of this class of intellectuals who rejected the entire Aryan heritage and sought to create a counter culture by giving a new identity to the *Shudra* and *Ati-shudra*.

Intellectuals before Independence could be grouped under these four broad categories in the entire social spectrum. At one end of the spectrum was the staunch revivalist Vishnubava Bramhachari and on the other was Agarkar, a pure rationalist. It can also be seen that if Jambhekar, Ranade and others could be, by Gramsci's classification, 'traditional' intellectuals, Jotiba Phule was surely what he called an 'organic' intellectual. (*Selections from Prison Notebooks*, 1991, p. 5)

One would have expected this intellectual tradition to flourish once political freedom was obtained. In fact, the founding fathers of our Constitution were inspired by these ideals. They set for the new nation the motto '*Satyameva jayate*' (Truth alone triumphs), which was taken from the *Mandukopanishad*. It was included in the preamble of the Prarthana Samaj which was inscribed on the plaque put up at the entrance wall of the building. The motto in reality is nothing but a universal, axiomatic truth. Had the founding fathers of our Constitution picked up an aphorism 'humanise, equalise, spiritualise' from one of the speeches made by Ranade at the Prarthana Samaj and reported in its official journal, *Subodh Patrika*, it would have been more appropriate for any welfare State that aimed at achieving social justice and universal brotherhood in a rightful, ethical way. However, not only did they fail to notice Ranade's message, their own hopes also were gradually belied. And with that declined the intellectual tradition in Western India, slowly but ceaselessly.

4

Have Intellectuals Become Redundant?

Do intellectuals have any relevance in our society today? Is there any place for them in society in an onward march? Have intellectuals abdicated their social responsibility or has society abandoned its intellectuals? If their relevance cannot be denied, then why did contemporary society lose interest in them? Moreover, why should this have happened to us? This is the principal focus of my reflections in the remaining part of this book. But before I do so, it is necessary to raise another question: whether intellectualism was really ingrained in India? Or was it a sort of Western transplant which failed to strike roots here? To a large extent it appears that the beginning of intellectualism here was not an organic process, but a mere transference of ideas through a kind of cultural induction. Many of the intellectuals of the period borrowed heavily from Western intellectual writers. For example, the two works of Thomas Paine, namely, the

Age of Reason and the *Rights of Man* were Jotiba Phule's favourites. Occasionally a Vishnubava Brahmachari rejected Western paradigms and value systems but was not successful in replacing them with indigenous ones. His ideas as expostulated in the *Sukhadaayak Raajyaprakarani Nibandh* could at best be called a kind of Utopian or Romantic socialism. Even if he was a contemporary of Karl Marx, he arrived at his thoughts on social welfare independently. However, his views on equality among all men and women as well as welfare schemes to be adopted by the State were only forays in the realm of Utopian thinking and did not have bearings on reality. His answers could be correct, but his method was unscientific, to say the least.

It is a noteworthy departure from the Western intellectual tradition that in India the members of the intellectual community belonged to a particular social class endowed with a right to education coming to them by accident of birth. This class of the so called 'high-born' were exposed to the Western concepts of liberalism, rationalism, nationalism and above all humanism. With a few brilliant exceptions the initial reaction of the newly educated elite was not against the traditional sanctions imposed on the 'low born' depriving them of social, cultural and even educational rights. The British rulers and administrators too initially did not wish to disturb the caste and class structure and consciously supported this dominant caste or class from reasons of self-interest. It is the ideals of the hegemony of this dominant group that were reflected in every aspect of society and culture for the latter part of the 19th century which is termed as a period of 'Enlightenment' in this part of India.

From Raja Ram Mohan Roy to Mahatma Gandhi, Dr. Ambedkar and Vinoba Bhave, our country produced a galaxy of social thinkers who were, in a sense, heretics as they defied the traditional order and sought to create a new order on the basis of rationality and equality. These I would term as 'amateur' intellectuals whose ideas ranged from constructive conservatism to radical rationalism, at times bordering on anarchism.

Gramsci who criticised the methods of traditional historical writing which was to him, 'nothing but the hagiographies of national heroes', developed the concept of 'history from below'. Much before Gramsci, it was Jotiba Phule, perhaps the first subaltern historian in India, who made a scathing attack on this monopolisation of the fruits of enlightenment by a particular class of Indian society, thus placing its members in an advantageous position and perpetuating them as a dominant class. If the members of the dominant class had genuinely felt uneasy about their unfair advantage and consciously worked to remove invidious distribution between man and man, and between man and woman, the history of modern Maharashtra would have followed a more enlightened path. But that was not to be. It was left to Jotiba to make a frontal attack against the sanctioned slavery in caste ridden Hindu Society and give expression to the discontent that lay latent in the hearts and minds of the oppressed. But by the time he came out with his vituperation against the dominant class for their exclusive rights, its members, empowered by the new University education had already leapt to high official positions, thus enjoying a double advantage, one accruing from their ritual status and the other from the official position. The bitter conflict that ensued between the privileged and the unprivileged constitutes the essence of the social history of modern Maharashtra. When this revolt against the exclusive right of the dominant class to intellectual property gathered momentum, the immediate reaction of the members of the dominant class was one of bewilderment and anger; for they had not anticipated challenge to their authority. Many of them, soon realising that their privileges could not really be justified, came to terms with the situation. Some of them, in fact, formed the vanguard of the movement for the upliftment of the less fortunate and deprived. Till recently Maharashtra was fortunate to have such leaders as N.M. Joshi, S.M. Joshi, S.A. Dange to guide the working class in its quest for social justice.

The reaction of the diehard members of the dominant class who were insensitive to the suffering of the Dalits, as the depressed came to be called, to the social revolt was one of hostility. They shunned the clamour for universal education, for it threatened the very foundation of their privilege. With the advent of freedom and popular sovereignty in 1947 this dominant class gradually withdrew from the social mainstream and retreated to its shell. It was sad to see these members of the intellectual class who provided leadership in the struggle for freedom, slowly losing interest in political happenings in India, and turning a blind eye to the vital issues concerning contemporary society. In an attempt to retain their separate identity, they either immigrated to greener pastures or withdrew into their shell and became impervious to everything that was happening around them. Such is, in short, the history of the intellectual class in Maharashtra.

A fortuitous assignment to write a history of the University of Bombay (University of Mumbai since 1995) provided me an opportunity to study the lives of those savants who made their alma mater proud by strengthening in a significant way the great academic tradition of the University, the only academic institution of its kind in the whole of the erstwhile Bombay Presidency for over a century since its establishment in 1857. While so doing they also made this great city a centre of intellectual pursuits. The city attracted all those ready to take advantage of the opportunities in commerce, education and administration offered by it.

Talented individuals rose to prominence and formed Bombay's 'urban leadership'. (*Urban Leadership in Western India*, 1972) If Mumbai provided intellectual leaders to the entire country in many fields of human endeavour for a sustained period of a century and more, the credit for it goes to these men who zealously guarded the intellectual nature of this otherwise commercial capital of India. Mumbai, as it is called now, was a beehive of intellectuals for over a century and was adored for this role too by the educated classes of other cities and Presidencies. Although it still enjoys a place of eminence, no person concerned about the city's general health can deny that the intellectual health of the city has of late declined. As a consequence its intellectual leadership is passed to the new urbanised centres like Delhi and Bangaluru or to its original competitor Kolkata. All too clearly scholars from Mumbai whose contributions are recognised by the rest of the world are dwindling in number. This is made more painful by the fact that there is no effort of any kind visible either at the official or the non-official level to revive the tradition of learning. In fact the process of de-intellectualisation in every field is hastened as those in the relevant professions have contributed, and are still contributing, knowingly or unknowingly, to accelerate the de-intellectualising. Signs of an intellectual decline are clearly seen in Mumbai's academia, media, and the literary and cultural fields.

Four areas that have suffered the most and are responsible for the de-intellectualising of the society around are the mass media, academia, and the worlds of literature and culture. It needs to be told that I do share the optimism of many, among them our former President Dr. Abdul Kalam. He has said:

> "Nations are built by the imagination and untiring enthusiastic efforts of generations. One generation transfers the fruits of its toil to another which then takes forward the mission." (*India 2020*, 1998, p. 21)

The city of Bombay was singularly fortunate in having at the helm of affairs throughout the 19th century, educated and enlightened men and women of exemplary social understanding who strove hard to instil in the city inhabitants a broad, liberal and progressive outlook. It was an exercise in social engineering at its best. Institutions of learning and research were set up, where various kinds of scientific and literary studies, including studies in languages and literatures and also of religious philosophies and comparative theologies were undertaken, publicly discussed and debated and even published for the benefit of larger audiences. Scholarly missionaries like Dr. John Wilson who arrived in Mumbai at a rather sanguine age and studied the scriptures of many religions debated with the local proponents many points of religious tenets basis of justice and fairplay. He and those who followed him made the university educated local youth rethink the tenets of their religions, whether Hinduism or Zoroastrianism or any other. But in the process they also interpreted these eastern religions to the West. Sir Alexander Grant, Vice-Chancellor of the University was one of the earliest scholars who, in a paper presented in a meeting of the Bombay Branch of the Royal Asiatic Society and later published in *Fortnightly Review* (Jan.1867) acquainted European audiences with the teachings and greatness of the poet-saint Tukaram, who has a place of prominence in the hearts of the local people. He was followed by Rev. Dr. James Murray-Mitchell, J.F. Edwards, Rev. Justin Abbot and a host of others. Interpreting and reinterpreting, evaluating and revaluating the living religious tradition was not only a lesson in religious tolerance but was also an indication that the society was maturing intellectually and was preparing itself for plurality of views and socio-religious practices.

The social clubs started by various communities exclusively or collectively for the express purpose of enhancing social intercourse, inter-cultural learning and understanding were manifestations of the same attempts that led to the flowering of corporate life in Mumbai. These community organisations which were soon to set the pace of social change provided platforms for the older and the younger generations to discuss and debate various issues of reform. It was a classic case of the regressive members of the society holding back the progressive over-enthusiasts, even as the progressive members pushing the regressive ones into accepting the change. These very organisations were later to play a significant role in the political struggle.

The cultural leadership of the entire society in the first half of the 19th century was in the hands of wealthy and socially aware businessmen who were basically leaders of their respective communities. Convinced of the need for formal education for the future generations, they promoted Western education. Little did they realise that they were doing this at the cost of their own leadership. The educated youth that came out of the portals of schools and colleges and later of the University were soon to replace the leadership of the old guard. The new intelligentsia of the city that included stalwarts such as Dr. Bhau Daji, Dr. Atmaram Pandurang, Deenanath Narayan, Mangaldas Nathubhai, Sorabjee Shapurjee and a host of others soon assumed leadership in every walk of life, social or cultural. They set up schools, supervised them, and occasionally taught in them. They also started organisations with specific objectives, built up their membership and drew plans for achieving their objectives. The very names of these organisations such as Students' Literary and Scientific Society, Buddhi Vardhak Hindu Sabha, Upayukta Dhyan Vardhak Sabha are indicative of their dedication to the spread of knowledge. This also marked the end of the era of businessmen leaders whose aim was giving back to society some portions of their accumulated wealth for public works. Philanthropy for social good was their main claim to leadership. The Rajabai Tower Library and the Senate Hall could be built on such munificent donations and so could be built many other monuments in the city such as the Frere Fountain, also known as Flora Fountain. However, their attitude towards officialdom and government at the same time was subservient, and the leaders of the younger generation were bound to detest it. They had to therefore relinquish their leadership to the succeeding generation which had absorbed more than superficially the values of Western liberal education.

Western education afforded local youth an access to books on Western philosophy, ethics, logic, economics and political science. It was an age of enlightenment for them, and the light seemingly had come from the West. In addition to the books on social and political issues by thinkers such as Edmund Burke, Thomas Paine, Jeremy Bentham, James Mill, John Stuart Mill, Herbert Spencer, the political histories of the nations of the world, the biographies and autobiographies of their leaders were also studied with interest by them. Little had the British government at the time anticipated that the promotion of Western education in India would instinctively draw the young minds to the precepts of European liberalism. Direct contact with various socio-political ideas of European thinkers worked like a touchstone and transformed a section of the community into a beehive of ideas and thoughts, alive to various ideological viewponts. The Anglo-Indian professors such as Professor Henry Green, Sir Edwin Arnold, Dr. William Wordsworth, Sir Alexander Grant, Professor F.G. Selby, Professor F.W. Bain, Professor Armine Wodehouse and a host of others who moulded the opinions of their students became indirect or direct catalysts of the social action and change. Sir Bartle Frere's seven Convocational Addresses as Chancellor of the University were enough to galvanise the students who heard them with a totally new enthusiasm. In the very first convocation in 1862, he had said:

> "I would beg of you to recollect that you are no longer pupils of any single school, but graduates of a University. Your standard must henceforth be, not that of your masters, or even of the government to whose service some of you may devote yourself, but of the whole educated world. I pray you that what is here taught is a sacred trust confided to you for the benefit of your countrymen. The learning which can here be imparted to a few hundreds, or at the most to a few thousands, of scholars, must by you be made available through your own vernacular tongues to the many millions of Hindustan... Remember, too, that not only the character of the

> University but the character of your whole people, is to a great extent in your hands." (*Speeches*, 1870, p. 111)

What inspiration such words gave to fresh graduates could easily be seen in the literary works published during the decades that followed. Books on natural and physical sciences, economics, history, religion and also literature were published in sizable number. During the decades following attempts were made to bring European knowledge closer through the regional languages.

When the initial feeling of awe generated by the new enlightenment subsided, the educated youth began to suffer an acute sense of anxiety. An invariably, facilely drawn comparison of the conditions in Europe and Britain with the state of affairs in their own country was bound to leave them discontented. The disparity between their country and that of the rulers became evident and the roots of social discontent were sown here. After the era of enlightenment, came the era of realisation or analytical examination. The educated young man began to think of the religion to which he belonged, of the rigid social structure around him and the miserable economic state of the society around him. Community leaders felt the need to start organisations or associations engulfing, not only their community, but also the entire society, for the welfare of the society at large. The new graduates believed that many battles would have to be fought to remove the darkness of ignorance and rid of social evils in the garb of religious fervour. If the second half of the 19th century saw many socio-cultural movements, the roots of the movements were to be found in the thinking and works of these men who belonged to the urban intelligentsia of the time.

Religious and social reform movements generally interact with one another. A revivalist trend was seen in Western India mainly due to the attempts at Hindu religious resurgence in the east by the reformist zeal and labour of Keshab Chandra Sen (1833–1884) who broadened the basis of the Brahmo Samaj, and Ramkrishhna Paramhamsa (1834–1889). The preachings of these focused the attention of the newly educated youth to India's great spiritual and cultural heritage and fostered in them national awareness and racial pride. These movements had a significant influence on the youth of Western India too. If the tenets of the Brahmo Samaj were direct imports from Bengal, those of the Arya Samaj were formulated in Mumbai, and, if they both were studied with interest here, it was the same kind of ecclectic fervour that was released from Western knowledge. Neither the Brahmo Samaj nor the Arya Samaj was seen taking real roots in Mumbai. In this sense, leaders in Western India could be said to have stayed away from much rethinking of religion. As it is such a rethinking was next to impossible in a multi-religious society; instead they pursued with social reform which aimed at removing the aberrations that had crept in their own ancient religion. Of course, their reaction to social change was different from their earlier generations and varied. There were those who did not like the new-fangled notions of the so-called 'light' from the West, and, about religious oppression they were happy to remain static. There were those who wanted social change for a better and just society. This rift gave rise to two schools of thought, coming into conflict with each other. All the members of the society found themselves, soon, in one or the other camps. As far as religion was concerned, either they were traditionalists or conservatives, revivalists or reformers. In politics they were either conservative or liberal. The class of revolutionaries was yet to arrive on the scene. Even radicals appeared much later. Though the camps were different and the methods dissimilar, all had a common objective—Renaissance. Curiously however, the leadership of the various camps in favour of change went, slowly and naturally, to academically sound, socially aware, and individually honest and sincere people. If one leader dropped out, no vacuum was created for long; there was someone else, equally great if not greater, to fill the void. This was the need of the time and a requirement of the situation.

While some were enchanted by the arguments of the revivalists, there were many others who reacted sharply to their religions plagued with superstitions, the deceitful behaviour of priests, the oppressive caste-system and excessive idol-worship. The more courageous among them, a few, were drawn to Christianity with its principles of humanity and catholicity and converted to the new faith. : Rev. Narayan Sheshadri (1820–1891), Rev. Vishnu Bhaskar Karmarkar (1834–1881), Hari Ramchandra Christie (1820–1865), Appaji Bapuji Yardi (1826–1894), Rev. Nehemiah Gorhe (1825–1895), Baba Padmanji (1831–1906), Pandita Ramabai Saraswati (1858–1922), Rev. Narayan Vaman Tilak (1861–1919)—all embraced Christianity of their own will and accord. The conversion of Narayan Sheshadri in 1833 caused in Mumbai a sort of a religious war. But at the same time when an educated, intelligent youth was attracted to a different religion on rational grounds, a need was felt to review, discuss and modify the tenets of their own religion. New studies of Hinduism, Zoroastrianism and the like began to be published at the time. A need was also felt to discard oppressive customs based wholly on superstitious beliefs. Religion, it was felt, should re-write itself on the grounds of humanity and justice. Women, it was accepted, deserved a fair deal, regardless of what the scriptures said. Child marriage and *Sati* system, it was concluded, should be totally discontinued. Widow marriage should be given social sanction and the caste-system should not be rigid, it was felt. Soon there came, one after the other, a host of social reformers who, alone or with others of similar thinking and inclination began to attack openly the oppressive customs of Hinduism and other religions. But the ancient Hindu religion was so lethargic that it required the power of many elephants to push it and therefore the pace of social change was dismally low.

If our intellectuals were working in the right direction, what prompted them to forsake that path? That the newly elected Government of a newly created nation should follow the path of social justice and think of new, affirmative actions for empowering the weaker sections, could not be faulted. But why were we in a hurry to right the wrong committed for centuries and expected a social *revolution* instead of social *evolution?* All knew for sure that social change had its own pace, that the affirmative actions of the government would at best marginally increase the speed of change. A social revolution overnight like political revolution is not possible. Then why was the miracle expected and why did every other leader, national or local, talked of social revolution?

On a very general level, one can say that if by middle of the 19th century a new life was injected into the city of Mumbai by enlightened leaders, the latter half was the period of reformers from the educated urban classes, as described by Christine Dobbin. Picking up the baton from them, if the leaders of the

20th century had made efforts to continue with social reforms, they would definitely have achieved more grass-root reforms, and might have been nearer in realising the dream of an equitable and just society. If they had succeeded in their efforts, then the country would have perhaps rested on a more solid foundation, socially and culturally. However, 1900 to 1947 was a period of brisk political activity. Obviously the struggle for freedom had to be given the priority it needed, relegating everything else to a secondary position. Those very leaders, who were the front runners in bringing socio-religious and cultural change, were seen leading political agitations of all kinds and velocities.

With Independence, several front ranking leaders unfortunately withdrew into a shell, perhaps with a gloomy conviction that the *real politik* did not suit their kind. These leaders of integrity withdrew from the political mainstream. And that started the decline of ethics in public life. Within a short period of time, the decline of political idealism and ideologies resulted in short-sighted political populism. It was inevitable. The post-independence leadership quickly adjusted itself to the new kind of politics while the old guard abandoned their role of leading from the front and were seemingly happy experimenting with pilot projects. The new leaders were not properly trained in theories of governance, nor were they groomed or well enough grounded in Western social thought. The obvious effect of the lack of an ideology was that a proper political culture could not evolve. The rules of the game changed drastically to revolve round personalities. The personality cult in due course became the only 'political ideology'. While we kept our democracy afloat the degeneration of political and public life became evident everywhere. It cannot be denied that the public-State interaction which is so very essential for any democratic system has unfortunately set the trend towards de-intellectualisation which had a snowballing effect in most fields of the public sphere. The intellectuals who have failed to perform their social function have created a number of difficulties for society. First and foremost, is the apathetic relations between this class and society at large and the latter losing respect for the former: In barely half a century, in independent India one finds a contemptuous attitude towards any kind of intellectual activity. It is looked down upon by the rulers and administrators as 'armchair criticism' or futile thinking.

To be intellectual is to be 'non-productive', is the slogan firmly ingrained in our minds. It sums up the social attitude towards the intellectuals in general; for, it is thought that intellectuals are the people who *consume* without *producing*, as they are not involved in any productive process, useful to the material progress of the society. At the same time, intellectuals in India comprising members of the teaching community, the creative artists, writers and publicists including journalists, social thinkers and commentators seem to have lost their will to become useful to the society in any positive way and have become self-seekers. The gap between what they preach and what they practise is awfully visible and exposes their hypocrisy. Perhaps it is for this very reason that their words do not carry the weight their predecessors did. Why should a feeling of guilt assail them when they undertake a critical appraisal of the things around? Alexander Herzen had passionately advocated that the prime function of the intellectual is to criticise. If the intellectual has to pursue this as his life-time job with no retirement, why should he abdicate his responsibility with disastrous consequences to the society?

One cannot be an effective critic without possessing a spirit of inquiry backed by a moral or ethical code of conduct. Just as necessity is the mother of invention, a doubting mind is the beginning of inquiry. The intellectual, of necessity, is a sceptic and scepticism is the root cause of change and progress. A sceptic will question prevailing religious tenets and tradition. However, a traditional, religion-based morality too—one which successfully keeps society together in a simple, uncomplex way—is badly needed today. The definition of religion may have undergone a change, but some kind of a moral order to hold a complex social system is imperative. Walter Lippmann, the liberal and intellectual editor who wielded considerable influence on American society in the early decades of the last century had suggested the creation of a moral order with intellectual postulates that demanded an attitude of 'disinterestedness' in the evaluation of morality. This he had called a public philosophy.

It is commonly seen that with the spread of the scientific spirit, people no longer seriously believe that they are governed by the heavenly forces. In our society, however, where religion is much more deeply intertwined in the day to day lives of people, conversion to modernity based on science and rationalism is indeed difficult to achieve. Even those who consciously imbibed the scientific temper struggle hard to reconcile rationality with emotion and spiritualism, make a clear choice between the head or the heart. C.P. Snow talked about the linguistic, emotional and attitudinal divides of two cultures: the scientific and the non-scientific. When our scientists too are seen consulting heavenly bodies for happiness and well-being, what wonder if many more such divides exist in our society, depending on attitudes to religion. If scientists lead life at two levels—one of traditional religiosity and the other of scientific temper, how can be the non-scientific community blamed for observing old religious tenets and taboos?

It is traditionally believed that university teachers, editors of newspapers, writers and artists are the intellectual leaders of a society, alongwith the political leaders, and, therefore, have a certain social responsibility. They are expected to perform their social function to the best of their ability. Our newly created nation had hoped to reconstruct itself along democratic patterns with the help of these intellectual leaders steeped in the European liberal tradition. It was hoped that these new intellectuals imbued with a new spirit would replace the old time sedate leaders. However, these groups engaged in the liberal professions have somehow belied that hope. Their failure has not only brought their own professions into disrepute, but has also been responsible for an overall cultural slidedown of society.

Discussion at some length is called for on what went wrong and why these four major influencing groups lost their hold. University and college teachers, editors, writers and cultural officials working in their respective fields of academia, media, literature and culture no longer are respected by society generally. In fact, they are looked upon as the 'enemies' of the society. My chief argument in the following discussion is that it is these fields that have let down society, and that their failure has brought us to intellectual bankruptcy and led to a de-intellectualised condition where little is expected to be generated except money. The worst aspect of it is that money thus gained through fair or foul means is spent on pure and unmitigated pleasure by exploring newer and newer avenues of amusement. In the acquisitive society that we are finding ourselves in, if intellectualism is not pursued along with the accumulation of wealth, there is every danger that we will relapse into exploitative feudalism with a democratic cover but with moral and ethical corruption intact. A society which till yesterday took pride in its ideal of 'simple living, high thinking' has degenerated into a society of 'high living, low thinking'. Years of indifference to any philosophy of a proper collective life has resulted in the utter collapse of civility. Belligerence of every hue and shade is on the increase in society, intensifying arrogance and intolerance in every field as its accompaniment. The lesson of moderation seems to have been forgotten in the land of saint-poets within sixty years of freedom.

5

The Gentle Art of Preparing the Curriculum Vitae

Let us begin at the very beginning. A lot of rethinking about higher education is being done at the highest echelons of the Ministry of Higher Education. Realising the importance of quality in higher education, more money is being allotted to education in the annual budget of the Government of India. New Central universities are planned. New courses of study are mooted. Capacity in every branch of study in every educational institution is increased year after year to accommodate more and more students wanting higher degrees. Apparently an entire generation is pounding the university gates for admission—a generation with diverse social and cultural background. And the universities are expected to train it for a life that is becoming more and more competitive and complicated. The specially appointed Knowledge Commission, the University Grants Commission under the Human Resources Development Ministry and individual university are expected to work out a formula to give 'quality' education to as many students as possible to achieve the goals of social justice. All of them have on hand an impossible mission. The winds of globalisation are forcing this new generation of students to ever remain on the edge of efficiency and competence in their chosen fields of activity. Gone are the days of leisurely study. The words of Clark Kerr seem to apply perfectly to the situation here. In his Godkin Lectures (1962), he said:

> "To the academician, conservative by nature, the sound made by the new generation often resembles the howl of a mob. To the politician it is a signal to be obeyed. To the administrator, it is a warning that we are in changed times..." (*The Uses of the University,* 1963, p. VI)

It is a welcome sign that the Government of India is taking serious interest in higher education and is wanting to raise it qualitatively. More and more corrective measures are being employed. However, there is no awareness of the reality at the State level. Expansion has taken place at the cost of qualitative improvement in higher education. Those in the education department of the government of Maharashtra are hardly disturbed at the pathetic performance of the younger generation of students at competitive examinations. How would they be concerned about the international ramifications of globalisation? Their efforts, mostly mooted at the official level as they are, are confined to the promotion of applied or vocational education. We had faulted the British educational system in India for being pegged to the objective of producing clerks and officials for government usage. Are we not doing the same, although with a difference? Have not our universities ceased to encourage serious debates and dialectics generating new ideas? The State Government is interested in spending less and less on research, whether in the social sciences, humanities or natural sciences, for such expenditure is considered unproductive. Social philathropists who are otherwise ready to provide funds for public charities are also not interested in funding research. As a result, our universities themselves have become large scale public sector enterprises interested in producing at best managers for industrial capitalist enterprises. They hardly provide the intellectual leadership to society. Not surprisingly, therefore, intellectuals could be easily dispensed with in such an atmosphere.

The real trouble started with our failure to define the goals of higher education at the outset. Our first Prime Minister Pandit Jawaharlal Nehru once said:

> "A University stands for humanism, for tolerance, for reason, for (the) adventure of ideas and for the search for truth. It stands for the onward march of (the) human race towards even higher objectives. If the Universities discharge their duties adequately, it is well with the people

and the nation." (*Convocation Address*, Allahabad University, 1947)

But it appears that these noble ideas remained only platitudes. If the Prime Minister of independent India knew what to expect from a university, why are the universities in our country reduced to mere examination boards and why are they run like government departments? The fact is that our planners failed to strike a balance between liberal education which was once the backbone of our education system, albeit a gift from alien rulers, and vocational education. We have gone in for a purely utilitarian approach to education and liberal education is lost sight of; subjects like Philosophy and Logic have suffered for 'want of students'. There are few takers even for the pure sciences. No amount of coaxing and cajoling the young ones helps. Why would students want to study something which has no market value and therefore such subjects have lost all attraction and respect? When education is confused with trade, commerce or technique, the contemplative disciplines are sure to fall through disuse. Moreover we refuse to learn from others' mistakes, why we refuse to learn from our own predecessors' mistakes. Professor Allan Bloom's *Closing of the American Mind,* on publication in 1987, caused ripples in American academic circles as he had attributed commercial pursuits instead of philosophic quest for truth or pursuits of honour and glory among the younger generations to the neglect of classical literature on the campuses. His indictment of the contemporary society in academia as well as society at large centred round the devaluation of Great Books of Western Thought as a sourse of wisdom. To him the failure of the centemporary liberal education has led to the inability of the students to fashion a life for themselves beyond the mundane offerings touted as success. To him education should imbibe in students a philosophy of life and that philosophy is learnt only through Great Books. One common reproach in our present education system also is that it fails to imbibe liberal values among students. Bloom's theory which is clearly understood when one reads the sub-title of his book—'How Higher Education Has Failed Democracy and Impoverished the Souls of Today's Students'—was debated in great detail in the U.S. campuses and outside, even rebuttals such as Lawrence W. Levine's *Opening of the American Mind* were published. We, however, meekly accepted the demise of liberal values in higher education and went in hurriedly for total 'vocationalization' of courses.

There is an interesting case in our own history. Among many Societies of Higher Learning established in Bombay was the Bombay Branch of the Classical Association which was started in 1912. The Association had eight branches all over the world and propogated the importance of study of Classical languages and Classical literature. The paper of Professor A. Ailinger of St. Xavier's College read before the Association had urged the University to give preference to Latin, Sanskrit, Arabic and Persian languages instead of French in the University of Bombay as French was not considered as a Classical language. There were many supporters to Professor Ailinger's argument which was similar to that of Professor Bloom. The University, however, did not relent.

In the post-Independence era, there was yet another catastrophe. Quality was sacrificed to quantity. The rulers were caught between two difficult options, expansion or development. We opted for expansion and utterly neglected development in higher education. Universities and colleges were opened without proper faculty and the requisite infrastructure, and the rulers wanted the common people to believe that this was development in the educational field. Successive chairpersons of the University Grants Commission started their tenures with much fanfare and publicity and ended with a whimper. The disease is diagnosed, the remedy is known; the patient, however, is not recovering because the proper injection is not being given! Despite the much advertised "rethinking" at the highest echelons of government, no change has been visible so far. Since higher education is one of the items of government subsidy, politicians who wanted to 'nurse' their constituencies, took extra care in opening new colleges and demanding new universities for their areas and allowing the already existing colleges to languish for want of resources. 'Social justice' by way of 'education for weaker sections' was their new *mantra* which they conveniently chanted. In reality, educating the weaker sections of society was a greater challenge for educationists, but it was considered an opportunity to build a political base, similar to opening sugar factories in Western Maharashtra. In the process, college and university education has lost its relevance and routinely churning our degree-holders has become the main objective. A government that plays with education pays the price in politics, literature and culture. And now not only the government but students also are paying the price. It is a pity that while education in our country is becoming more and more impersonal, politics is becoming more and more personal. It would have benefited both if the reverse was true.

In Maharashtra, the office of Chancellor of universities of non-agricultural as well as agricultural, by convention vests with the governor of the state. The experience is that since the Governor has more pressing issues to be attended to he can hardly devote time to the problems of higher education in general and the universities in particular. He, willingly or unwillingly, but heavily, depends on his secretariat for suggestions and advice. His over-dependence on a couple of officers in his secretariat is seen to give rise to the formation of lobbies and cliques that at times rein a new Vice-

Chancellor's enthusiasm and innovative urge and make him or her a cog in the official machinery. When lobbies and cliques start containing independent minded Vice-Chancellors and aim at controlling universities, no change is possible. Cliques and lobbies, being of a negative tendency, are generally made of statusquoists. Every time a change is contemplated it is opposed either by the bureaucrats or by the ministers and, as Alexander Pope would say,

> "And unawares Morality expires.
> Nor public flame, not private, dares to shine;
> Nor human spark is left, nor glimpse divine;
> Lo! thy dread empire, Chaos! is restored; ..."

(*The Dunciad, 1853,* Vol. III, p. 152)

Many a problem could be averted by making the universities truly autonomous with no state intervention of any kind. A beginning can be made by allowing the universities to appoint their own Chancellors whose individual stature will bring status to the academic institutions. And they will have sufficient time for academic issues and, more importantly, have interest in running the University. Otherwise, the indications are that no amount of minor remedies will improve the present system of higher education. The decline in higher education can be seen right from the selection of Vice-Chancellors. If there is a continuous decline in the stature of Vice-Chancellors, should not at least a part of the blame be attributed to the state government? The Maharashtra Universities Act 1974, made the office of Vice-Chancellor a full time, salaried position. It was quite logical, for educational expansion could no longer be trusted to social stalwarts who held top honorary positions in the University and were otherwise free to pursue their own interests or vocations. With the rapid expansion in higher education, universities required men and women to be available on the campuses all the time to solve academic and non-academic issues. But making the position full-time and salaried should not have been construed as academically and administratively a step up the ladder for university teachers. The rationale behind asking aspirants to *apply* for the coveted position of Vice-Chancellors cannot be understood, apart from the fact that receiving applications from so called eminent persons gives a vicarious pleasure and sense of superiority to the bureaucratic machinery of the State. In such a situation ill-treating Vice-Chancellors becomes a kind of an entertainment in which both the education minister and the departmental secretary don the robes of ring masters and have a field day. Together they can make life miserable for an occupant of that august chair if he persists with his purely academic attitude they dislike. And it is very easy to do so as it is they who hold the strings of the purse and grant permissions of all kinds. They would like to see a small, subservient person ready to gulp all official affronts to remain in the big chair for the tenure of five years. Things have reached such an alarming stage that a person from nowhere suddenly comes to occupy the Vice-Chancellor's chair as he has mastered the art of preparing an impressive and fat *curriculum vitae* (in total violation of the meaning of the phrase) and has acquired the skill of wire-pulling (euphemism for cosiderations of caste, locality, highly placed relations etc. which are totally extraneous considerations). Those few with self-respect not only do not apply for the position, they do not accept it even if it were offered to them on a platter. Why do good, competent people decline the Vice-Chancellor's chair? This should, in fact, be a cause for concern for the education minister and the Chief Minister. Rarely is the right person seen occupying the right position these days. Should not the framers of the education policy or whoever recommends educational reform mull over this fact: why the best men and women are not willing to accept Vice-Chancellors' chairs? The malaise, perhaps, starts from here and percolates to the other ranks.

This leads to another question, similar in nature. The Vice-Chancellor is not only the academic and administrative head of the University, but he is also a leader of society seen at socio-cultural gatherings and, who, by his independent and mature reasoning and sane advice helps enhance the intellectual level of the society. If this is so, what should be the qualifications prescribed for him? Surely, that he should be an intellectual himself, of independent thinking, a father figure with mature reasoning and every inch a democrat and liberal? If this is expected of him why not invite exceptionally talented people to adorn that august chair, bringing glory to the position they occupy?

The fact is that the Vice-Chancellor's position is no longer considered a position of honour. Firstly, it has become careerised, as the highest university office for which one has to apply and compete and even play the politics that is required to be played by candidates, and their political mentors. And secondly, the position is sufficiently governmentalised. Those who occupy the position stand exposed as their political games are known. Many self-respecting persons have remained away from this position as they do not wish to apply and compete. If the government and society underestimates its real greats or ignores them, it is their loss. The State Government can be faced with how and where to find persons of academic leadership and impeccable integrity and credibility. But the Selection Committee should be able to do the 'head-hunting' job, it should at least know the who's who of society. Appointing a judge or a high government official on the Committee may not always be the proper way. The University Acts only enumerate the responsibilities of the person holding position and judge suitable candidate by scrutinising paper qualifications. And here lies the real travesty of higher education in India. Technically all are equal before the law of the land, but can the principle of equality be stretched even for filling up top public positions in the society? Then are we not removing the difference between 'first class' and 'pass class' by putting everyone in the 'second class'? If professional experience is measured only in terms of, say, the number of years of service, and if one's ideas on social justice, and his comprehensive view on education are not taken into account, will it be a proper assessment of one's abilities? Will it not be the application of wrong criteria? Equality of opportunities is equated with equality in results! In fact, such application of wrong criteria is practised by the rulers in all fields, and this constitutes a major reason for the decline of standards. Added to this, are the extra considerations of caste, community, religion and, of course, candidate's amenability. Once these considerations become all too important then ambitious mediocrity rules the roost and the mediocrities, who fill the high offices, subsequently start taking a vicarious pleasure in suppressing the creative urges of teachers. This is a real danger to society. Some high positions in society should be above mundane considerations and treated as similar to those in the government for which there is no wire-pulling and horse-trading.

The idea behind appointing a Pro-Vice-Chancellor to assist the Vice-Chancellor in a large University that has become unwieldy has in reality resulted in creating parallel centre of power. One sees a University as a battle-ground where the Vice-Chancellor has to work extra hours in countering the moves of a Pro-Vice-Chancellor eager to occupy the top chair at the earliest, much before his time to do so. The concept has failed miserably and calls for a rethinking on whether an administrative head such as a Proctor could make a difference. That would leave the Vice-Chancellor free to attend to academic matters only.

Re-producing ill-digested passages from text books in examination is not the real test of students, just as a B+ Grade at Graduation, Post-Graduation, or a PhD degree does not and should not really qualify a person to be a college teacher. But successive governments have attempted to define everything in quantitative terms, even qualifications or the number of years of experience. One year's experience repeated ten times cannot become ten years' experience, but it is considered appropriate qualification for the post of Principal of a college! The administrative ability of a person, his vision of higher education and his charisma that encourages students to achieve have been of no avail. The state government with full control on education tends to ignore such points. There should be an 'administrative audit' of the Principal of a college. A Principal's yearly performance should not be left to the Management to assess. Even teachers should have a say in the assessment of the Principal's performance.

Academic rigour, exactitude of mind, expression, command over the language of instruction and, most importantly, the ability to think, are the characteristics of a creative teacher. The present system is more concerned about paper qualification than ability, as the latter cannot be measured by a foot rule. This is not dissimilar to the physical stock taking of books in a library. For many librarians, perhaps, a book is a book, and nothing more. Putting one and all in the second class, may be the easiest way of assessing answer books or evaluating a candidate's performance in an examination. Even a pass class or failed candidate can be promoted; but does it not do injustice to a truly meritorious candidate? No system today desires to take note of this. It has been well proved that obtaining degrees may or may not be the real test of a student's knowledge. In the absence of a better testing technique, the present form of examination has to be continued. But the real issue is whether a Ph.D. degree is really required for teaching undergraduates? Awarding Ph.D. degrees the way it is done, is nothing short of making a mockery of the old debate of teaching and research. Career advancement of individuals is, perhaps, confused with academic advancement. Publish or perish, is Americanism at its worst and it is being seriously reconsidered in the Western world today. Here is yet another case of refusing to learn from others' mistakes. In 1940s a committee was appointed in the U.S. to find out why the best men of society do not opt for the study of literature. The findings of that committee would be an eye opener for any society, for the committee said:

> "The very best men of society do not opt for the study of literature at all. The next best drop out at the end of a year's experiment. The mediocre, at the end of two years! Those unfit, survive and become Doctors of Philosophy who go forth and reproduce their own kind." (N. R. Phatak, 1947)

Had we learnt a lesson from this report would Ph.D. degrees in regional literatures have become a subject of social derision? In Mumbai today any criticism of the academic scenario falls on deaf ears. The concerned decision makers pat themselves on the back for 'universalising' education which was once the prerogative of a select few. Mass scale expansion is, no doubt, a commendable feat for a nation of our size and social complexities, but for how long should they continue taking the credit only for expansion? 'Higher Education for all those who seek it' should be an avowed principle of any government. But the presently imparted higher education can, by no stretch of imagination, be called 'higher'. It awards degrees, gives a mental satisfaction to millions of young students for being degree holders, but if a degree-holder cannot write a casual leave application, or any application or formal/informal letter for that matter, then of what use is that degree except mental satisfaction? If a first class achiever becomes a teacher on the strength of his paper qualification but is afraid to go to the class and face students and therefore finds a new excuse every time to postpone taking lectures—is he not unfit for the profession? No amount of outside support is going to help him. He will have to study the subject himself, improve his public speaking skill, if he is to be an effective teacher. It is high time universities introduced a course in public speaking and methods of teaching—on a voluntary basis initially. The ability to think and theorise, linguistic accuracy, knowledge of the subject, teaching ability, exactitude of mind—these along with the normal academic qualifications should be the criteria on which a teacher should be selected. These, however, have become relics of the past. Research degrees today are more useful to a teacher in building up his career as they ensure his place and reputation in his subject. In the absence of yardsticks to measure these abilities of people aspiring to be teachers, we are giving excessive and undue importance to Ph.D. degrees and published 'research' papers, instead of refereed research articles in serious, academic journals. In the absence of academic and scientific journals, articles published in any periodical or journal of indiscriminate standard go to 'pad' the *curriculum vitae* of a teacher; and then it becomes difficult to evaluate the worth of these articles, which only adds to the confusion by blurring the difference between the first rate and the second rate. Unlimited hypocrisy and unqualified pretending resulting in academic frauds are the children of an inferiority complex. But they are common among University teachers these days. I know of a certain teacher who used to put a big notice on the blackboard at the entrance of the main gate of the college informing his students and to the world at large that he would be taking extra classes for the benefit of his students, but who almost simultaneously never failed to put up another typed notice on the college notice board that he would be unable to take the extra lectures announced by him due to some unforeseen difficulties! Needless to say, his preference of putting the "end" above the "means" took him up to the Vice-Chancellor's chair. How can we ignore our common experience of seeing these days a Ph.D. degree holder doing his research in his academic adolescence and then vanishing into the teaching fraternity never to be heard again? This degree, by far, is generally considered in the world of learning to be the researcher's initiation into research, whereas more often than not it becomes his first and the last attempt at research. Yet he continues to enjoy its benefit throughout his career. Evaluating theses has become the gentle art of making enemies. It could also enable some to make lifelong friends who soon become accomplices in hush-hush academic frauds. Academic sticklers are soon thrown out of the system. Goof–ups in theses often become subjects of gossip in the academic circles but nobody wants to displease anybody.

Extending one's *curriculum vitae* year by year is a popular game today, indulged in by many a member of the academic community. There does not exist a more hollow claim than "attended numerous national and international seminars", for 'numerous' could be just two and 'attended' does not mean 'participated'. Even when one claims participation it does not indicate the quality or the extent of participation. The anxiety of the college and university teachers to make career moves through promotion is understandable. There is nothing wrong in legitimate ambition. But unqualified and unabashed ambition cannot be justified. A story is told of Justice M.G. Ranade who was denied promotion to the Bombay High Court Bench for quite some time. At a public meeting a speaker made reference to this 'injustice' done to 'the prince amongst graduates', as Ranade was generally called. The saintly intellectual is reported to have said to him after the meeting was over that questions of salary and promotion are not subjects of public discussion. Such was the level of public morality then. Today we focus on hardly anything but salary and promotion.

The real trouble started with the bureaucrats nursing a feeling that the college teachers had a smaller work load compared to that of government employees. That the teachers have to prepare for their lectures was forgotten. With increased work load of teachers, thus, the first fruit was that the disappearance of time for preparing lectures. With salaries being paid through the Government Exchequer, every Education Minister and Secretary has taken pleasure in adding to the workload of college and University teachers. Credit can be taken by the authorities for introducing what is in grandiose terms called 'academic audit'. Academic audits based on the submission of reports of activities is deceptive, to say the least. These reports can sometimes pass off as humorous writing. Teacher assessment by students too could be misleading. Such an assessment could be just one clue in the yearly performance of a college or University teacher.

The undue importance given to 'national' and 'international' seminars by National Accreditation and Assessment Commission (NAAC) has led to the proliferation of such seminars. Invite a professor from a neighbouring state and the seminar is qualified to be called as 'national'; induce a foreign scholar on sabbatical in Mumbai to participate in a seminar and it can immediately become 'international'. For sure this happens not in all cases but it does in many. And what happens to a seminar organised locally in which the reputed city academics participate? It remains 'local'!

A word about the evaluating and rating agencies and their processes like NAAC and ISO (International Standards Organization) that are rapidly becoming popular among the Mumbai colleges. However well intentioned these rating agencies are, their criteria of rating do not necessarily convey the correct picture of the academic standing of the institutions. They give more consideration to physical structures. College and university buildings are spruced up before their visits. This is good because teachers get better physical amenities. The physical aspect is important, no doubt. But when you take a number of criteria into account it leads to fallacy of composition and therefore misrepresentation. The academic criteria binding them induce teachers to 'pad' their 'academic' achievements. Such self-deceit in academia calls for introspection rather than inspection.

6

Nothing Succeeds Like Excess

Like the academia, the media too play a major part in intellectualising or de-intellectualising any society. Euphemistically it is called the Fourth Estate of democracy, although our Constitution recognises only three—Parliament, the Executive and the Judiciary. Credible media in any democratic set up carry out the responsibility of being *vox populi*—the voice of the people. It is like a social trust, and therefore it is that media are attributed with the sobriquet of Fourth Pillar or Estate of society. The written word always has the power to impress. In the new situation however, when multi-media appear to be ruling, the written word is perhaps losing its imporance. Literates—particularly neo-literates—who had tremendous faith in the written word, making the print medium wield power which frightened even the most powerful. This power is now seen being usurped by the electronic media. But before the increasing power of electronic media is discussed, it would be rewarding to understand why the power of the print medium is corroded and why it is instrumental these days in de-intellectualising society. The fact is that the written word no longer enjoys the sanctity it did a couple of decades ago. There are many reasons why the print medium no longer effectively carries out the responsibility that is entrusted to it in a democracy.

That the face of Indian journalism would change drastically after independence was but expected. With the sole objective before it, namely, gaining political freedom, achieved, our newspapers overnight found themselves without a purpose, for there was no need to run newspapers with the same missionary zeal as during the fight with British rule. The press then had played the role of a powerful vehicle of thought. Even after the goal was achieved it still continued to be an influential and effective carrier of opinion necessary to propagate the ideas of the leaders of a new nation. Newspapers could play the traditional role of being the watchdogs of society, and keeping a vigil on erring ministers and public servants entrusted with the task of reconstructing the nation. They tried to play that role as sincerely and faithfully as they could in the early years of independence, but in a democracy of masses without education, with unlimited hypocrisy becoming evident in every walk of life, the print medium found itself at cross-roads with the new purpose. The newspapers found themselves struggling for survival. They were forced to accept the ghastly reality of commercial element in the production of newspapers, for no longer was it possible to survive on mere high thoughts and lofty words. Once the commercial aspect of newspaper production became real, they found it obligatory to cope with four types of pressures —pressure from politicians whose retention of political power largely depended on the continued ignorance of the masses; pressure from the advertisers whose strong lobbies had interests in the management of 'convenient' news; pressure from readers who were oft and on victims of emotionalism and intolerance; and, lastly, pressure from the proprietors who, by the ever increasing governmental restrictions found it difficult to publish newspapers day by day. The editor whose obligation was to face these pressures had to be content with the residual freedom. Even that residual freedom was not negligible for him while directing and supervising his newspaper as well as voicing straight and honest opinions on affairs of public importance. But the democratically elected governments soon came to realise that they stood to gain only by curbing press freedom. Therefore they were uneasy even with the residual freedom enjoyed by the editors of newspapers. The editors should fall in line and help showcase politicians' successes, they thought. The need to advertise their successes to the masses was essential to suppress their misdeeds. The easiest way to muzzle the press was to tax newsprint and to extend financial boosts through advertisements to those who wholeheartedly supported governmental actions. It did not stop at that. Still some went ahead with launching their own newspapers. Newspapers were started without proper ideological profiles. Professionalism was a victim in the process of monitoring news and newspapers this time started facing a crisis in credibility. When a new lesson was learnt that entertainment took up a major part of people's lives, a new component was added to the newspwper's objective, which now became 'to inform, to educate and to entertain'. It is difficult to guess at what stage the 'entertainment' component made its entry in the print media. But it is certain that it was a later interpolation.

With the old value structure collapsing and professional pride and integrity yet to be inculcated at the societal level, newspapers mushroomed. Though initially the spurt in the newspapers was hypocritically considered as a sign of a strong Fourth Estate, the increase in the number of newspapers made competition stiff making their survival doubtful. And then, all of a sudden, 'marketing' became all important, like any other commercial product in the market. The baffled, harrassed editors still stuck to their guns, but the marketing managers, more attuned to ghastly reality, saw in their writings vanity and hypocrisy of bygone era. The new marketing managers had scant respect for high-sounding rhetoric of the 'leader writers'.

Within a span of three to four decades after independence newspapers changed a lot. Old, closeted editors who commented and criticised objectively and disinterestedly as detached yet concerned observers, slowly found themselves out of tune with the goings on around them. One by one they became relics of the past, and vanished in the thin air. Under the garb of modernity, commercialism entered the journalistic world and newspapers, particularly the tabloids, tended to overplay selected events under pressure of competition. This resulted in setting aside one by one almost every tenet of classical journalism. Comments began to be cleverly camouflaged in news, opinions began to be loaded, but a sense of duty and propriety was, however, lost. Increase in circulation and advertisement revenue was all that mattered. The new lesson learnt this time was that everything sells if you have a perfect marketing strategy. Truth sells, and so do lies, if effectively worded. Vulgarity sells and so does obscenity, if attractively presented. And all this under the garb of freedom of the press, a right guaranteed in the Constitution. The principle of plurality of views was given the go by under the pressure of vested interests, thus becoming another casualty of the sly assault on the constitutional rights.

As idealism slowly vanished from the lives of people, it vanished from newspapers too. During natural calamities of national dimensions, the newspapers did come together, but otherwise the same event was reported differently by different newspapers. They attacked the weakest links in the governmental machinery, but showed allegiance to the powerful. And when the jolt came in the form of internal emergency (1975–77), they did not know how to react. Not being habituated to any kind of repressive measures the new generation of editors did not possess any fighting spirit. They did not have the language of bold confrontation and interrogation either. The earlier editors were fighters, used to fighting of censorship and repression bearing even punishment of internment for subversive political writing. But they had already become history. As one national leader described them, the new editors were only asked to bend, but they started crawling. In the two years of the emergency, newspaper proprietors and editors learnt a yet another valuable lesson—survival before duty. Never was the journalistic world the same again. Those romantics who took upon themselves the responsibility of keeping a vigil on democratic functioning were soon to polarise politically like their counterparts in the civil services, the police department and, to an extent, even the judiciary. Undoubtedly, the print medium was facing a crisis in identity, but the gullible readers ever ready to swallow whatever came their way were unaware of this transformation. Many of the newspapers, particularly the language newspapers which catered to neo-literate or semi-literate readers, thrived on sensationalism. They drew their strength from political conflicts and intra-party factions. The so called scoops were veritable mines of individual conflicts and mutual settling of scores. The obvious outcome was that the power of the printed word diminished with every new generation of readers. Every new generation, exposed to more than one source of information, lost faith anew in the printed word.

The tenet, 'everything sells if you have a perfect marketing strategy', found multifarious extensions in all fields and walks of life, making a mockery of our experiment in democracy. For it gave rise to the doublespeak that George Orwell talked about in his novel: *Nineteen Eighty-Four*. The doublespeak which initially took the form of camouflaged falsehood (remember the surrogate advertisements of yesterdays? The beer company with its all too known brand name advertised as a producer of mineral water, or as a manufacturer of bottle opener!) did not take time to degenerate into unashamed hypocrisy. Too many players in the market prompted aggressive marketing. With aggressive marketing all the rules of journalism changed one after another, with quick intervals or sometimes even simultaneously. The earlier rule of journalism, 'the higher the circulation, the higher the advertisements, and the higher the revenue' was replaced by 'the higher the circulation, the higher the losses'. Does it sound healthy for society and for the profession of print journalism, if a newspaper proprietor, in a meeting of senior editors, says that 'newspapers are *for* advertisements', and further, 'by giving news in it you add value to it'? An editor in the past was supposed to be 'a mender of souls', 'a moulder of opinions' and 'an educator par excellence'. But a strong willed proprietor today can sell his newspaper without appointing an editor and still be commercially successful! Many might remember the quarter page advertisement published a decade or so ago, mentioning all the 'necessary' qualifications for a candidate wishing to respond to the advertisement inviting applications for the position of editor: that he should be able to lead the team, should be an innovator, ready to experiment and so on, but the punch line was, "he need not write". Till then, it was considered essential for the editor of a newspaper to be a good writer, a craftsman of words, being a specialist in a subject or two, and a generalist in as many subjects as possible. It was also accepted that he would be concerned about the welfare of society. The earlier generation of proprietors at least believed that the miniscule minority did read the editorials however pompous they were, but they also believed that the miniscule minority was that of opinion makers. Today's proprietor openly takes an anti-intellectual position as he is convinced that 'no one reads editorials'. The situation is both a reflection of the editorial writer's lost hold on society, as well as his own failure to write in the compelling style that would induce readers to read the editorials; and also his employer's new but unfounded conviction that readers are no longer interested in any serious reading. The proprietor perhaps is conveniently overlooking the fact the editor today has to dish out three types of fare to his readers: what the readers want to read, what the advertisers want readers to read and, most importantly, what the editor wants readers to read. In some cases the editor's position is deliberately kept vacant, so that none could oppose the crass commercial intent of a newspaper proprietor.

To make matters worse, there are many television channels today that want a share in the advertisement revenue of newspapers. The obvious result of such a medley is that so many stake holders are running after so few advertisers that no one will even think of supporting academic, serious journals or, for that matter, even literary journals which have gone out of circulation one after another due to heavy financial losses. The television channels have become tools of entertainment, pure and simple. Being young this medium is yet to frame its rules and is content to cater to a large community that prefers to be caught by the heart rather than the mind. That accounts for the emotive serials that innocently propagate regressive beliefs and customs, and wipe out all the good work of our reformers. Raising TRPs is their sole objective and 'survival of the fittest' is their only mantra. Their definition of survival includes mottoes such as 'kill the competition at the earliest' and 'grab the market share'. What is more objectionable than this entertainment medium is that the print medium with its tradition of nearly two hundred years is seen unnecessarily competing with the electronic media and is seen resorting to cheap gimmicks such as 'guest editor' and 'page-3' concept with reports on the epicurean lifestyles of the glitterati, shown in larger than life images. If the most successful newspapers refuse to discuss serious social issues and resort to reporting socialite evenings or highlighting modelling dysfunctions, Bollywood musings and religious festivals with a sprinkling of semi, pseudo or mock serious articles of the shortest possible length, then what happens to their role of taking up causes, informing and enlightening readers? Can they be said to be enjoying power without responsibility which according to Rudyard Kipling is "the prerogative of a harlot"? If the electronic media sensationalises an incident under the garb of search for truth, the print media trivialises a serious issue. Thus both are instrumental in attracting people's attention away from real issues. It can be granted that an average Mumbai citizen's daily routine is so gruelling that he tends to seek moments of pleasure or light amusement. All channels of television are catering to such needs of the society in the daily soaps and reality shows. But why should the print medium too cater to these needs and happily accept the responsibility of de-intellectualising society? 'Entertainment' is the key word of society today, and the media feel obliged to provide just that. The new brand of editors has misread the entire situation. These journalists feel happy evolving a formula that gives their readers or viewers pure pleasure that nurtures epicurean tendencies of people. Along with the ever growing middle classes the epicurean tendencies too are growing. The editors of newspapers and television anchors by resorting to the new success formulae achieve instant publicity.

Mark Lilla, quoting Socrates, mentions a special category of men whom he calls 'philo-intellectual terrorists' and describes them as:

> "...those who enter public life not as rulers, but as teachers, orators, poets—what today we would call intellectuals. These men can be dangerous, for they are 'sun-burned' by ideas. Like Dionysius, this kind of intellectual is passionate about the life of the mind, but unlike the philosopher he cannot master that passion; he dives headlong into political discussion, writing books, giving speeches, offering advice in a frenzy of activity that barely masks his incompetence and irresponsibility. Such men consider themselves to be independent minds, when the truth is that they are a herd driven by their inner demons and thirsty for the approval of a fickle public. Those who listen to such men,

> usually the young, may feel the stir of passion within; this feeling does them credit, for properly channelled it might bring honour to them and justice to their cities. But they are in need of an education in intellectual self-control if they are to turn that passion exclusively to good use." (*The Reckless Mind*, 2001, p. 211)

One does not have to look anywhere else, for this description expresses today's situation aptly. History has taught us that unbridled passion is among the worst deterrents of an intellectual life in modern society.

There is a great divide between the English language press and the regional language press. The English language press in Mumbai or the 'National Press' as it is called, is, to borrow Plato's expression, 'twice removed' from (local) reality', as it shows more concern for international events than local issues and happennings, whereas the language press as the regional press is called, finds itself at a loss to grasp issues of national and international ramifications, mainly due to its lack of wider exposure and deficiency in the English language. A journalist of today has to be at least bilingual; for those working in the English language newspaper, proficiency in English and fair knowledge of the State language is necessary, while for those working in regional language newspaper, along with the proficiency in the modern Indian language in which the newspaper is published, a fair knowledge of the English language is essential

The media today, both print and electronic, is, knowingly or unknowingly manipulated by the high and the powerful and manipulate the de-intellectualised society. Real issues that need immediate attention are overlooked as they require hours of study. A wedding extravaganza in a celebrity family acquires a fairy tale proportions and the Cricket World Cup frenzy kindles instant jingoism in young and old. And there is none to bell the cat. The print medium has over the decades developed some conventions and taboos which serve as guidelines for it. The electronic medium is so young that it has still to evolve its rules. It is still struggling for survival as too many players have entered the market, and not all of them are purposeful. How long this situation will last is anybody's guess. In these days of struggle for survival ethical code and social responsibility are on low priority. Like the print medium, the electronic medium too is over protective of its freedom and will not accept a code of conduct drawn up by any outsider. It will result only in losing business. Who will bell the cat, then? Who will contain the electronic medium? And the print medium too, in the meantime, struck by the impact created by the electronic medium, is seen aping it. Only when a majority of the members of the electronic medium feel the need for such a code, can worthwhile change be expected. At present however, copying with slight variations the innovative programmes of competitors to strike a formula of success, and in the process allowing no one to succeed, has become the rule of the game. Almost every newspaper or television channel is seen slavishly copying the innovator, helplessly and abjectly.

The media is a powerful carrier of thought. It is an effective instrument for intellectualising a society. But today it is at a loss to carry out its responsibility and is more interested in 'entertaining' readers or viewers. The written word has already lost some of its influence over society as its credibility too has suffered due to its secret, ignoble hankerings of people, its excessive coverage of ordinary happenings and its lack of courage to tackle the serious issues of national importance. It is true that such a state of affairs cannot last long. But at the present moment, their operation is acute. Both newspapers and television channels are taking up anti-intellectual stances and in the process are taking society on a cultural slide down.

7

Where Silence Is Golden

The third category of intellectuals that have belied our hopes constitutes the professional writers. Before dwelling upon the question as to what social function a writer serves in a democracy, it is better to begin with a question: why does a writer write? If this question is asked of writers—poets, novelists or playwrights—their answer mostly would be that they write for pleasure, or to give vent to inner urges; or to calm down their disturbed minds. Such feelings may be perfectly sound in their own way. But then the reply does not answer the question: why does a writer 'publish' his creations, and more so why does he make them available to others called readers? This means it is not only for pleasure or purging his inner self of disturbance that a writer writes. Then does he write for money, name and fame? Every human being and that includes the writer, has the full right to aspire for a name and fame and even money, from his communicating his experience to others around him. There is nothing wrong in such a legitimate ambition of which any decent person need be ashamed. G.H. Hardy, the British mathematician, lists three laudable motives which lead men to prosecute research. These may well be applicable to the writer too. According to Hardy the three motives are: first, intellectual curiosity, a desire to know the Truth; the second, professional pride, anxiety to be satisfied with one's performance, the shame that overcomes any self-respecting craftsman if and when his work is unworthy of his talent; and finally, ambition, desire for reputation, and the standing, even the power or the money that it brings. (*A Mathematician's Apology*, 1941, pp. 18-19) Creating a work of literary art is one thing and publishing it is quite another. Publishing a poem, or a novel, or a play has a motive other than just honouring one's obligation to oneself, and cannot be deemed unnatural. Yet the fact remains that publishing a work of literature in the form of a book or for that matter any other form, gives it another dimension that refutes the writer's claim that he writes purely to please himself.

There are of course, writers who do subscribe to the 'pleasing oneself' theory. T.S. Eliot, poet and critic of acclaim who has much theorised on his self as poet, undoubtedly will pass as the prince among such self-limiting writers. Some writers may extend the limitation to confessing that they write for other writers or those closer to them. In fact, Eliot is on record as saying, "The more serious authors have a limited, and even provincial audience, and the more popular write for an illiterate and uncritical mob." Eliot's ungenerous remark about popular writing might have been from hostile reactions to his own writings by the common readers of his times. But what, perhaps, Eliot really meant was that the more popular writer addresses a mass audience largely innocent of literary training and without critical standards.

Whatever it is, it is obvious that when a writer prepares a literary work for publishing, there is always an additional motive in mind than just pleasing himself or herself. It is true that many a time the writer attempts to write for an audience limited to one's own admirers; it is also true that on occasions one writes for the audience one does not know and at whose sensibilities one can only guess. By and large, novelists and short story writers write for a hypothetical audience.

For the writer who makes a living from his profession of writing, this perhaps is an essential condition. This leads us to yet another question: Is there any relation between the writer and the society round him? If there is one, what is it? Is the writer, due to the nature of his work, alienated from society? Or is it sufficient for a modern-day writer to be a narcissus of sorts?

If it is accepted that a writer writes and publishes his work for 'communicating' or 'connecting' with members of the society in which he lives, the argument leads us to the further question: does the writer who writes for the society around him have any social function? In other words, does he as a member of the 'privileged' class have any social responsibility? In a culture which possesses a true spiritual unity—or even a unity in diversity for that matter—a culture in which men and women are united or divided along emotional lines or in other ways, and yet share a common dream, the writer remains aloof, as if standing on a pedestal. He can afford to be solitary and cultivate his thoughts from his innermost self, for he can take it for granted that on larger issues he is united with those around him and so can go on to explore his own individuality through the characters he attempts to portray in his literary creation. There can also be a situation when the common dream has become dissipated, and the world of objective sanctions and values is lost. In such a situation the writer is forced, to re-gain a sense of unity with his own people through some abstract system consciously worked out and create his subjective, collective as well as individual values. Cleanth Brooks in his Kerr Memorial Lecture of 1965 on *The writer and his community* sums it up thus:

> "How else can a writer function? With dozens of problems of selection and emphasis and articulating to make on every page that he writes, he cannot be always looking back over his shoulder to try to catch the changing expressions on the faces of a hypothetical public."

A writer cannot create a literary work in a vacuum. Undoubtedly, he should be endowed with two qualities, viz. creativity and craftsmanship. His creativity and craftsmanship are the result of his understanding of the 'tradition' of the society around him and his 'individual talent'. Whether his literary creation is 'an emotion recollected in tranquillity', as Wordsworth describes poetic expression, or 'a heated caprice of an agitated mind', as a novel can be described, both the inner forces drive a writer while he is involved in the literary activity. Just as 'what is said' is important, 'how it is said' is also equally important. 'What is said' depends on the ability of the writer who temporarily assumes the role of creator, while 'how he says it' depends largely on his craftsmanship, a quality which he has acquired. If he is a gifted writer, creativity would come to him naturally, while his endeavour to communicate with others effectively would depend on the level of technique acquired in craftsmanship. Even his creativity is a combination of his understanding of the 'tradition' he inherits, consciously or otherwise, and the 'individual talent' that he has acquired through his study of man and Nature. Like T.S. Eliot, many writers and poets have tried to define 'tradition'. A literary work, creative or discursive, is, thus, in the ultimate analysis, a comment on the contemporary society and as such the writer is a social critic. A creative writer too in this sense is a social critic and this precisely is the social function of a writer.

All literature, in a sense, is contemporary literature just as 'all history is contemporary history'. Tradition plays an important role in a creative work, in prose or poetry. In discursive prose it does so prominently. Tradition, by definition is partly constant, and, therefore, unchanging, but partly changing. By making use of the knowledge of the past of his society, inherited over generations, the writer assumes the role of conscience keeper of the society. His constant evaluation and re-evaluation of the tradition he inherits, makes him a preserver of old values that are worth preserving and also the creator of new ones, thus discarding those that are worth discarding. In the process, he becomes the principal agent of social change. It must be remembered that there is nothing sacrosanct about tradition, that is, social mores, conventions and customs. "Conventionality is not morality", said Charlotte Bronte emphatically in her classic work: *Jane Eyre*. The only exceptions are the basic human values such as compassion, forgiveness, universal peace and truth. Apart from these, the conscience of the writer, like that of other human beings, also changes. It deepens with new enlightenment. New values based on newer concepts of equality and social justice are created; and the writer is, has always been, sensitive to such changes resulting from concepts and ideas of social justice in the widest sense of the term, and also those dealing with science, religion and philosophy. As a socio-cultural leader of the society, it becomes, therefore, his responsibility to keep these human values alive by constantly bringing them before his readers. He needs to assure his readers that any kind of discrimination on account of caste, creed, race or colour is an affront to human dignity and a crime against humanity. He has to convey to his readers that complete equality may be hard to put into practice, but not equality of opportunity. The writer must strive to project and portray this concept at least in his imaginary world of literary creation. He must prepare his readers to discard what is irrational, irrelevant and dead in the tradition and accept new values by applying the criteria of reason and social good. For, the social good presupposes a living, changing society. If he is a consummate artist and a thinker he may become a forerunner of the shape of things to come. The larger the area of his influence, the better it is for society. It is a proven historical fact that an intellectual revolution invariably precedes material revolution. Emerson said that "every reform was once a private opinion". An idea takes its birth in somebody's fertile brain and when it is diligently delivered, grows into a movement. This, I believe, is the process of creating new values. The writer who is a hero unto himself thus tends to be a role-model for his reader-admirers.

The ideal writer does not belong to any particular class. He is detached and stands aloof from the rest of society by choice, not by compulsion. For his own professional reasons he prefers to be the 'outsider', 'a spectator'. Of course, he cannot stay a total stranger to his social milieu. He can at best be termed an inner 'outsider'. He prefers to be left alone but he does not suffer loneliness. Why, one may ask? He is a social critic and as a social critic, of necessity, he is a recluse. To discharge his duties effectively he has to maintain a critical distance from the society around him. While the extent of 'critical distance' is debatable, the need for objectivity is indisputable. John Fowles, the American novelist and essayist, has discussed his inspiration to write. He goes to the extent of saying that 'he writes therefore he is'. In an essay titled, 'I Write Therefore I Am', he says echoing Descates that his avowed ambition has always been to alter the society he lives in:

> "Society, existing among other human beings, challenges me, so I have to choose my weapon. I choose writing; but the thing that comes first is that I am challenged." (*Wormholes*, 1999, p. 5).

Fowles's views could be those of any writer who today takes to writing professionally. He feels that the writer has three politico-social obligations. First, he has to be an atheist. Second, he should not belong to any political party. And third, he should not belong to any bloc, organisation, group, clique or school. As he says:

> "The first because even if there is a God, it is safer for (the) human mind to act on the assumption that there is not (the famous Pascalian *pari* in

> reverse); and the second and the third because individual freedom is in danger, and as much in the West as in the East. The virtue of the West is not that it is easier to be free here, but that if one is free one doesn't have to pretend, as one behind the Iron Curtain (has to) that one is not." (*Warmholes*, 1999, p. 10)

The writer, unlike the politician, is not in for a popularity contest. The politician has to remain an insider and has to play to the gallery to retain his position of power. This is not the case with the writer who has to be true to his own self and, at the most, to society. The writer is supposed to set standards and even utopias in the hope that they will be realities in not too distant future. All human progress has been achieved in the pursuit of utopias. The socially conscious writer has to be in that sense a spokesman of the nameless, the faceless and the voiceless who are generally covered by the Gramscian term 'subaltern'.

Ideally every work of literary art to be effective should be a carefully crafted provocative polemic. It must stir the reader's head as well as heart, that is, both reason and emotion and in some extreme unbearable situation, it must earnestly harness the horses of reason and unchain the tiger of emotion thereby leading to social change. In the case of the French Revolution, it was Voltaire who harnessed the horses of reason and it was Rousseau who unchained the tiger of emotion. It is the duty of the writer, therefore, to give expression to the discontent that lies latent in the hearts and the minds of his community, that is, his readers.

That the literary life in our society in the post-Independence period has languished cannot be denied. And it has happened despite the freedom of expression guaranteed by our Constitution. This constitutional guarantee offers exemplary freedom to writers, journalists and artists. Fortunately in the history of independent India there have been no serious attempts at secession or the suspension of these rights, with the sole exception of the days of internal emergency (1975–77). During this period writers' freedom of expression was sought to be curtailed, much to the chagrin of thinking people. Not used to facing repression of any kind, writers were so baffled that not many of them came out to fight for their fundamental rights and preferred to observe silence. Why were they so timid about displeasing the authorities? The reasons are many and varied, but not difficult to enumerate.

The first and foremost reason of the writer's complacency or timidity, whatever it is termed, is to be found in the decay of the democratic set-up. The causes of the deterioration of the young democracy of India are many, the foremost being the degeneration of political life. Numerous political parties, whatever their professed objectives, have, in a short while learnt to thrive on corruption and hypocrisy. There is a total absence in their thinking, of the concept of healthy and stable relationships. Also there is no consensus among them on basic national issues, though the leaders of every political party appear to be chanting the mantra of 'social justice'. Stable relationships between the political parties and a common minimum agenda on national issues are the prerequisites for any healthy democracy. Corruption has also thrived from the fact that the political parties, irrespective of differences in the colour of their flags, are guilty of the same hidden, ulterior motives. The objectives of these parties often do not even include capturing power, whereas the attainment of power should be the goal of every political party worth the name. Highly personalised politics has become increasingly a baneful feature of the Indian democracy. In her attempt to capture total and absolute power, Mrs. Indira Gandhi as Prime Minister curtailed freedom of expression, hastened the decay of political institutions, the decline of constitutional authority and public morality, which in turn laid the foundation of the criminalisation of politics. Political decay inevitably leads to cultural decay. In the absence of enough avenues for the upward social mobility of its citizens, 'politics' in any democratic set-up becomes a 'gainful' full-time profession. If an individual avows personal loyalty to a successful and powerful political leader, his or her political career is guaranteed, at least for the time being. Politics in India has become a profession which has no stakes but has all the chances of abundant windfalls of money. It has become a profession that allows, protects and ensures power, for personal prosperity. Once personal loyalty is given overriding preference over political and other ideologies, political power is attainable through patronage, money and muscle power. Success gained through political power breeds more such successes which further lead to more political power. This power not only corrupts but also intoxicates. Corruption and its cohort, the intoxication of power, make it further necessary to resort to criminal tactics for their retention. In such a situation the common man is a helpless victim. A writer's vocation expects him to oppose such wrong-doings. If he tamely abdicates his responsibility to society and ceases to perform his social function, then is he not a traitor to his calling?

In such a situation democratic principles degenerate into mobocratic tendencies. Will Durant has rightly remarked once that "Democracy without education means hypocrisy without limitation." ('Decadence of Democracy', in *Pleasures of Philosophy*, 1929) Failure to contain the explosion of population, failure to educate the masses, improper priorities and incorrect strategies of social welfare, corruption and excessive greed have resulted in the ever-sliding quality of our socio-cultural life where over half the population lives in sub-human conditions and is deprived of the fundamental rights guaranteed by the Constitution. The masses with their characteristic native wisdom, have not taken long to discover the hollowness in the words of newspaper editors and writers, and in the platitudes in the speeches of our politicians.

Our democracy, which has virtually turned into mobocracy, has thus tended to make uniformity a surrogate for equality and social justice. We have achieved some degree of success in reducing the traditional social inequalities that had crept into the social structure and in curbing idiosyncratic, arbitrary and exclusive elements. However, our democracy has also misguided the masses who have become the principal support of our national polity and who are also, consciously or unconsciously, helping the profit-crazy marketeers. It is the rabble that is often seen deciding everything. 'This is what the people want', is the refrain of today's marketing *gurus*. Everything has become a market-product and to sell it requires a marketing strategy, whether it is a cake of soap, a newspaper or a literary work. Even individual talent has to be marketed to be successful. Leadership appears to have lost its character as well as an enlightened vision and the will to lead. There is a pressing need for an appropriate leadership empowerment. Democracy the way it is practised in our country seems to minimise the obligation to lead. The demagogues who instigate the ignorant masses are catapulted into power by popular prejudices and, as seen recently, by hatred. It is the hatred of something rather than love, regard or friendship that unites people.

When political authority is weakened, writers are expected to come forward to assume intellectual leadership and lead the way to the desired social and cultural change. But that is not seen as happening in our society today. The decline in political culture surely affects the life in a society. Artists and writers in such a situation are expected to revolt against a corrupt system, thus helping, directly or indirectly, the rejuvenation of the society concerned. This is their social function. This has happened in Western countries time and again. Writers should lead a silent revolution through artistic creations or literary works. By depicting a debased society, making the protagonist express dissent and fight against the corrupt, polluted system, and by suggesting remedial measures they should endeavour to bring about the desired change in the social mind. The writers need not every time take to the streets waving placards but they must appeal to the conscience and reason of their readers. It is a common experience in Western countries that art flourishes during and after a time of war and literature has vigour even under the most despotic of regimes. Our writers have never faced despotism. Neither have they been ever subjected to repressive tactics in the recent past nor have they faced or experienced war in its full fury. Their experience in this respect was limited to two years of censorship during the internal emergency even then the repressive apparatus could not operate efficiently as the ruling bureaucracy was either corrupt or apathetic or simply insolent. Even in this singularly abominable situation our writers did not, rather could not, stand up to the severe test. To write in plain, vigorous language and make penetrative analyses of the abnormal situation one has to think fearlessly and fearless thinking and politically correct behaviour are incompatible. A majority of our writers today prefer to play safe and remain aloof and silent, in a sterile equidistant position from all political parties. Equidistance from all is not equivalent to non-conformism. One does not need to wait for the arrival of a Hitler or a Mussolini or a Stalin and wake up only after the State apparatus shows its totalitarian nature by its extreme repressive measures. World history is full of instances when the rulers resorted to silencing the voices that protested against the atrocities of the despots. Khalif Omar, after the capture of Alexandria, when requested to spare the library, is reported to have replied, "If the books in it are consistent with the Koran, they are superfluous and should be destroyed. If they are inconsistent with the Koran, they are harmful and must be destroyed." Despots before and after Khalif Omar have been the enemies of free thought, belief and expression. Therefore, the writer at all times should remain vigilant and resist even impending attacks of any sort on freedom of thought and expression. In modern times, even a mass society that pulls up men in authority can play similar role. "A society becomes totalitarian", says Orwell in *The Prevention of Literature*, "when its structure becomes flagrantly artificial, that is, when its ruling class has lost its function but succeeds in clinging to power by force or fraud. Such a society, no matter how long it persists, can never afford to become either tolerant or intellectually stable." (*Essays*, 2002, p. 939) Are we, in India, far behind this situation?

Few will have cause for dispute with Orwell's assertion that, "there is no such thing as genuinely non-political literature, when fears, hatred and loyalties of a directly political kind are near to the surface of everyone's consciousness". (*Essays*, 2002, p. 938) No writer, true to the integrity of his vocation, can really remain aloof from political happenings. He cannot keep away from controversial issues. "Even a single tabu" according to Orwell, "can have an all-round crippling effect upon the mind because there is always the danger that any thought which is freely followed up may lead to the forbidden thought." (*Essays*, 2002, p. 938) The writer in India today is still ignorant and perhaps even innocent of the kind inhuman acts and cruelties which a despot could resort to. For he does not have its first hand experience. The European and Russian psyche knows it too well as most people in those countries have undergone horrendous war experiences. Our writers have generally shunned politics, particularly after Independence. There are few 'thinker' writers who are either political activists or who run non-governmental movements. Antonio Gramsci, the Italian political thinker, faced imprisonment; Marc Bloch, the French historian of the *Annales* School, was arrested, imprisoned, harassed and ruthlessly shot by the Nazis point-blank; Anna Akhmatova, the Russian poetess, was not allowed to publish her poems in her life-time. It is their defiance of totalitarian regimes that have essentially made writers like Sartre, Camus, Orwell and Arthur Koestler all time greats. It is such Western thinker-writers who stood firm upon their ideals in the face of overwhelming odds that stimulated a spirit of critical inquiry in all aspects of human life and gave rise to a thought process that shaped the European mind; this generated rational-liberal ideas. And these ideas to a large degree account for the fall of the Berlin wall, the reunification of Germany or the disintegration of the Soviet Union. This is not to suggest that what is happening in Europe today is ideal or wholly conducive to human welfare at large. Admittedly, self-enlightened interest has been, and will remain a guiding principle in all human affairs. The point which is sought to be made here is that creative thinkers and writers are expected to respond to the challenges to basic human dignity and rights and play a crucial role in shaping the minds and thoughts of rulers and ruled alike, especially in a democratic set-up. This kind of response is unfortunately fragile in our country as compared to the West.

How the European writers zealously guard their hard earned intellectual freedom is illustrated by the protest led by the international writers' association, the PEN, against the German government's proposed law to ban pornographic literature in the late 1940's. Erich Kastner, a respected author of the Weimar generation, reminded his countrymen then that a similar legislation in the 1920s had made the simple, gullible sections suspicious of literature and had thus prepared the way for Hitler's book-burnings and exhibitions of 'degenerate art'. Kastner described this law as "a new Trojan horse".

Our writers in contrast, appear to assume mass society has no place for active protesters, free thinkers and creative personalities. Our society too, has neither the desire for independence and originality, nor can it distinguish a sane voice in the clamour for personal economic gains. The writer feels that if he does not join the chorus, he will not be heard. If the writer falls in line and expresses, so to say, pro-establishment views or, at least, observes a convenient silence over controversies he may be allowed to be, like many others, a partaker of government largesse and other material advantages such as memberships of various government committees or government awards. This is an attitude no less selfish than the argument that it is the duty of the government in democracy to support writers and artists, in the absence of yester years' kings and princes. In a democracy just as it would not be wise to stay away from governmental machinery, it would be just as much a mistake to award the government the role of a patron. The reponse that the writer is making in such a situation is one of convenient silence, under the pretext of 'critical distance' from society and government. Government patronage in the form of awards, subsidised housing, memberships of various official committees and such other benefits has in a democracy like ours an anaesthetic effect that is keeping writers in a permanent state of inaction and, willingly or unwillingly, more willingly than otherwise, they are seen succumbing to petty temptations.

There are many other reasons that keep the writer away from carrying out his social responsibility. Mass literacy seems to have lowered than raised the general level of culture and sensibilities. Obviously the majority of people who have learnt to read and write during the past fifty years have not received the kind of education that at least brings social awareness, if not enlightenment. The vast expansion of so-called higher education also, has led to a catastrophic lowering of academic standards. An attempt to achieve universal literacy is no doubt laudable. But can those who formulated and implemented educational policies, and the recipients of such education, take pride in the current situation? What passes for scholarship today is only an adjunct of power. Genuine teachers, scholars and intellectuals capable of disseminating knowledge have become redundant and idea-mongers whose principal talent consists in their ability to play to the gallery have become respectable and popular. Besotted by their lust for worldly success and desire to win popular applause, our modern day social critics have generally degraded learning and thus betrayed the noble calling of independent thinking. The disorientation of society, the indiscriminate expansion of mass-media, and the aimless growth of higher education have all contributed to the dilution of the quality of our intellectual life. With a few exceptions the performance of our intellectuals and writers has been generally characterised by self-interest, opportunism, cowardice, intellectual dishonesty and irresponsibility. This is tantamount to self-deception.

The courage to question seriously and on well reasoned ground the majority opinion in a literary creation constitutes the distinguishing mark of a social critic. Unfortunately most of the times he, like the politician, is driven by the 'correct' marketing strategy and does not want to be on the 'wrong' side. The present day social commentator seems to have almost forgotten that freedom of expression actually means the freedom to oppose, to criticise what he thinks wrong.

He appears to have relinquished his expected role of swimming against the current when the occasion demands it. Instead moulding the opinion of readers and creating new values for their consideration and for acceptance by the society at large, he finds it safe to uphold the old value structure, and resist change which is but a short step to obscurantism.

The writer's lack of courage to lead his readers rather than be led by them has inevitably resulted in his almost conscious efforts not to offend the powers that be. He has forsaken his role of a social critic and prefers to maintain an ominous and, one may even say, a studious silence about the literary merit or otherwise of a controversial book or of a socio-political issue. On such matters he tends to be non-committal, a position that guarantees him psychological safety. Such a critic is however quick to defend his cronies. This smacks of narrow, unethical groupism devoid of any altruistic intent. Such writers readily take up their pens where their own caste or community affinity, geographical affinity or group affinity is threatened. Even on issues concerning freedom of expression, they prefer to remain silent for fear of offending the high and the mighty. If a professional colleague is under surveillance or is harassed by the police for 'heretic' writings, and if he does not belong to their group or caste, they tend to ignore it or dismiss it as his 'personal' problem. Our present-day writers do not see that any attack on intellectual liberty and on the concept of truth, threatens in the long run every department of thought and that, therefore, freedom of thought should be zealously guarded. The writer's convenient posture to avoid the displeasure of powerful politicians is bad enough. But his abdicating his role of a social critic is far worse. The writer today does not enjoy the sound reputation he did in the past, because he has surrendered his moral authority. Few can today make writing a full-time profession as it cannot provide for a reasonably decent living. The book market in India has not grown as it should have been precisely for the reasons cited above.

Since most of the present writers in India are comparatively well-paid teachers or technocrats, they do enjoy, in the garb of academic freedom, a certain amount of freedom of expression. They, however, restrict their radical views to the precincts of their respective institutions. They remain studiously silent on public platforms for fear of incurring the wrath of the powers that be. In regional language literatures these days including Marathi, any significant or controversial remark, statement or claim made by a worthy or unworthy writer, goes generally unchecked, unchallenged and unregistered. There are no serious debates on any issue. This is a sure index of the writers' abdication of their social responsibility.

The moral authority of the writer gives him the strength to lead even the lay readers. Once that authority is abandoned no one would look up to him to say - 'Lead, kindly light'. In a rational-secular age, when God is conceived as truth and a moral and ethical code, newer norms of social ethics come into being to regulate human life. The story of man has essentially been one of eternal quest for an equitable and just society. Apparently there are two different kinds of morality—private morality and public morality—that is, morality in private life and morality in the public sphere. In fact though, both are two sides of the same coin. One cannot flourish without the other. Every new generation of a society provides for its members new standards of virtuous character, value based performance, and just social arrangements which are generally called relationships, such as father and son, mother and daughter, mother-in-law and daughter-in-law, husband and wife, teacher and student, brother and sister, brother and brother, sister and sister, employee and employer, friend and friend and so on. In all their forms, they are subject to interpretation. The social critic in the writer is expected to do everything on the high principle of human good. He has to be humane, democratic and secular. He should be in a position to offer a rational explanation for the causes he takes up. Every society, at whatever stage of progress it is, shares some common principles, at least in theory. Morality is one of them. Norms of morality, though not basic human values, have been ever changing, in response to new socio-economic dictates. Writers, including artists, are to a large extent, responsible for preparing the people to accept the changes for social good. There are some things relating to change that can be argued and debated. Since the writer is instrumental, to a degree, for such a change, he is expected to participate in the debate and stoutly defend the ideas he stands for. He has to enunciate and propagate some kind of value structure without indulging in propaganda. Such polemics is part of the writer's profession and the tragedy is that this is exactly what he is shying away from.

Popular ethos and social pressures in a mass society are enslaving the weak writer. Market forces and often rabid public opinion are seen pressing with enormous weight upon the mind of the individual including the writer and that has weakened him. When human beings grow alike, they not only lose individuality but each one of them also feels feebler than all the rest. Made uniform by the vast collective forces of the modern world the average individual becomes feebler, and even narrow minded, bigotted and dependent. The writer is no exception to this general rule. Candour and independence of opinion which constitute the outstanding features of the writer's profession are rarely to be seen today. It is this candour and independence of opinion that often makes him sound idiosyncratic, but his strength lies in his moral authority. If the writer's liberal outlook is sacrificed at the altar of the mass-society then he becomes an agent rather than a dispeller of oppression and repression.

Orwell, who, in his essay on "The Prevention of Literature", had grasped the situation in a totalitarian state, was of the opinion that:

> "Poetry *might* survive in a totalitarian age, and certain arts or half-arts such as architecture might find even tyranny beneficial, but the prose writer would have no choice between silence and death. Prose literature as we know it, is the product of rationalism, of the Protestant centuries, of the autonomous individual. And the destruction of intellectual liberty cripples the journalist, the sociological writer, the historian, the novelist, the critic, and the poet in that order. In the future it is possible that a new kind of literature, not involving individual feeling or truthful observation, may arise, but no such thing is at present imaginable. It seems much likelier that if the liberal culture that we have lived in since the Renaissance actually comes to an end, the literary art will perish with it." (*Essays*, 2002, p. 941)

Orwell, perhaps, has overstated his pessimism. In any case, he was discussing European societies and their cultures. In a multi-religious, multi-cultural nation such as ours, our physical existence will depend upon the continuance of a tolerant, liberal and humane spirit of the masses at large. In fact, it could be construed as the social responsibility of the writer to propagate timeless and universal values such as compassion and tolerance. If liberalism dies and is buried, a multi-cultural society such as ours will face new problems rather than solve the ones it is already faced with.

★★★

The City of Mumbai has been continuously under strain since Independence. In fact the strain was felt from the end of the Second World War when people flocked to the city from every nook and corner of the country. It continued to provide employment as a new boom had set in. Industries grew, the city pulsated with new life, and even its northern limits were continuously extended. Mumbai came to be known for commercial expertise, became the chief industrial and financial centre of the country with a disproportionate share in the key economic activities in the national economy. The Reserve Bank of India naturally came to be housed here, along with the head offices of most of the national and international banks, other economic and financial institutions and industrial houses. The expanding city became the vanguard of national economic progress and with it grew its cosmopolitan look. This role of the commercial capital of the country had been more or less thrust on the city because of a combination of fortuitous circumstances, partly historical, largely cultural, but essentially geo-political. It was no wonder then that the population of Mumbai grew in geometric proportion, from approximately 1.8 million in 1941 to three million in 1951, to 4.2 million in 1961, and to six million in 1971 to 12 million in 2001. By the end of the first decade of the 21st century, it is expected to cross 20 million. This multitude is accommodated in an area of 600 and odd sq. kms. Mumbai has seen expansion in floor space index at regular intervals, and now it can grow only vertically. Even marshy lands are filled, the sea is pushed back time and again, creating as much physical space as possible and yet more than half its population is compelled to live in shanty colonies under sub-human conditions. To say that the city is bursting at its seams will be an understatement. The experiment like of building a twin city, Navi Mumbai, failed to ease the pressure on civic infrastructure. There is already talk of the second Navi Mumbai. The continuous influx of migrants into the city from all the States of India was an invitation to transforming the city's cosmopolitan society to a mass society, but a society lacking diversity, unlike the 19th century when various communities had retained their diverse identities, yet were more united than at present. Mumbai society over the years has become a society in which the national or global influences on social and personal life such as the mass production and the mass media have stripped its citizens of their intrinsic diversity. One could call the

'Bombay brew' which is a queer mix of a variety of cultures—Marathi, Gujarati, Hindi, Kannada, Tamil, Telugu, Malayalam, Bhojpuri, English and so on. In filmi parlance the language that is spoken in Mumbai is called 'Bambaiya Hindi'. One may even find the responses of Mumbaikars to events, disturbing or festive, similar. A Mumbaikar is by and large aloof, yet concerned. He is disturbed, yet apparently unruffled. He has learnt to be tolerant, but when he is really agitated, he takes to the streets and does not hesitate to pelt stones. These are all signs of a mass society. In a mass society, similar likes and dislikes, similar opinions and attitudes, similar habits and mannerisms, similar activities including similar sartorial choices and similar emotional responses are shared by a majority of the population that becomes less and less diverse either as individuals or in terms of social class. Such a population has a tendency towards conformity. A powerful advertisement campaign can easily influence its hordes. In such a milieu where populist slogans find instant response, a powerful media and demagogy reap the benefit. The true aims and objectives of higher education become ineffective, as serious debates and discussions are detested, and there is unwillingness to accept new ideas. Yet there could be changes in fashion and clothes almost every day. In fact there is a tendency to shun anything that has a stamp of intellect and individuality. A box office hit film or an election campaign or whatever, pandering to emotionalism easily brings the desired results, as a mass society craves for escapes to a make-believe world. That this should have happened to Mumbaikars is unfortunate, but the great work done by the earlier reformers seems to have been almost thrown to the wind. More unfortunate is the fact that no the groups appear to have any desire to change the situation, whether they are teachers or litterateurs, media magnates or political leaders. Perhaps all have lost the will to do so or have become insensitive to their real responsibility towards society. The post-independence years for Mumbai have been years of neglect and belied hopes. Mumbai has been to successive governments in Maharashtra and Delhi both, the goose that lays the golden eggs. For want of proper care and nursing, this goose has aged prematurely. Till the dawn of the 21st century the city bore a worn out look. But of late its vibrant nature has evolved resilience. The Central Government as well as that of the State are showing some concern for the city, may be international pressure is at work.

Following the linguistic reorganisation of states in other parts of India, the city had seen a public outcry for the inclusion of Mumbai in Maharashtra. Mumbai was included in Maharashtra and also made the State capital, only after an agitation in which over 100 lives were lost. If the 1950s, therefore, was a period of successes and failures and claims and counterclaims in Maharashtra State, the 1960s was a seed-period as under the able and far sighted leadership of Chief Minister Y. B. Chavan, foundations were laid for many ambitious projects, which could ripen only in the 1970s, the decade of resurgence that witnessed a kind of cultural and literary flowering. The commercial Marathi theatre began to be frequented by even the non-Marathi audiences of Mumbai. And so was its experimental theatre. It was realised that commercial and experimental trends are like parallel currents and that the one reflected the emotional quotient of the society while the other its intellectual or rational quotient. The lesser the distance between the two parallel currents, the richer the society culturally. Marathi theatre in the 1960s and the 1970s was the envy of non-Marathi theatre goers from the other states. Playwrights, poets, novelists, artists, theatre and film personalities, musicians and singers made Mumbai, their dreamland—an abode, temporary or permanent. Mumbai was, in short, a happening place. Most of the artists were totally devoted to their art forms and strove hard to scale new heights of artistic excellence. The 1970s also saw protest movements in literature. Dalit literature which could be termed, in Gramscian term, the Marathi subaltern literature or 'the literature from below', opened new vistas for other genres of socially relevant literature such as *graameen* (rural) literature, women's literature, *kaamgaar* (workers) literature, Christian-Marathi literature, which prompted ongoing debates and discussions on paradigms for evaluating literary works. The resurgent decade saw the impact of stalwarts in almost every field, the media, academia, literature, performing arts or the fine arts. Many of them could be termed intellectuals as they had achieved excellence in their respective fields, were concerned in their own way, tried to mend the society around them and each of them had a constituency of his own where he made his impact. The 1980s in Maharashtra saw a slide down that necessitated for everybody including the political leaders, a pragmatic approach for securing one's own future. The 1990s were testing times, with bomb-blasts, communal riots followed by terrorist attacks or threats of such attacks. The city of Mumbai was humbled, to say the least, and life in the city appeared unsafe. Thus the Utopian 1950s, the realistic 60s, the resurgent 70s and the pragmatic 80s were followed by the nervous 90s. Its indomitable spirit makes the city tick even in calamities, natural or man-made, but the cultural resurgence of the city may take many years. With intolerance growing as a fall out of growing social and personal tensions, and suspicion and violence increasing, the sense of belonging so very essential for concerned civic sense is on the wane, causing harm to the culture of this great city. What went wrong with Mumbai? Why did the culture of ideas slowly vanish from the city? Why did it lose its intellectual leadership? Why is anything that has a stamp of the world of ideas shunned by its citizens? Who is responsible for such a pass? Why do the intellectuals who are still holding the fort, find themselves powerless and without any impact on Mumbai society? Why do they find themselves as a miniscule minority? Why does even the State Government which parades itself as 'the most progressive' government ignore them? What can be done to retrieve the situation? Can Mumbai lead the country again in socio-political and intellectual fields? How? These are some of the questions that need to be addressed before a remedial measure can even be contemplated.

8

A Culture in Search of A Policy

Social change precedes cultural change. The mature intellectualism of the sizeable section of society is an essential condition for social change. Social change is an onward march towards progress, for a change can be only horizontal, while progress implies vertical growth too. Social progress entails the coming together of a variety of forces in society, the foremost being enlightenment through education. Social change always proceeds along evolutionary lines. The government with an avowed and proclaimed policy of social justice can act as a catalyst, can enact and enforce laws to the effect. Enforcement of laws these days does not bring the desired result, as it is seen that, like cobwebs, laws catch small flies but let wasps break through, making the enactment look ludicrous. Appealing to the conscience of the people, thereby educating them about the desirability of change is the only sure way to bring about the expected result. And who can appeal to the conscience of the people? Not the film-stars or the sportsmen who today appear to have become the only role-models for the younger generations, but the teachers, the editors and the writers. In fact this is their traditional role and there is no reason why they should abdicate it. Cultural change requires the efforts of generations. Therefore any government that intends to bring about cultural change must initially concentrate on the intellectual health of the society.

Had the Government of Maharashtra taken care to help some credible autonomous committee formulate a comprehensive and integrated cultural policy for the State, formulate policies for language and literature, books and public libraries, heritage, along with a progressive policy for the performing and fine arts and other relevant spheres, it would not have lost the initial lead gained by the various Boards such as the Board for Literature and Culture that were established soon after the formation of Maharashtra State in the 1960s for promotion of the Government's progressive ideas. It should have encouraged setting up of 'Think-Tanks'. It is a shame that the State Government did not take the lead in the setting up of even a single institute of advanced studies in Mumbai during the last sixty years. Compare this with Delhi. How many advanced centres of learning have been created in Delhi during the same period? What is done to maintain the old ones that were established earlier? In fact Mumbai once prided in its

'Bombay Schools' of Economics and Sociology. Most leading economists and sociologists of the country were either teaching at the University of Bombay or were its alumni. Today one has to think hard to come up with the name of at least one Bombay University scholar in any of the faculty at the University or a Marathi writer with national or international standing. Should the State Government be faulted for disbursing insufficient grants to these institutions whatever the reason? For distributing meagre amounts of grant, belatedly, to a three-tier educational system which is not dissimilar to distributing poverty?

The trouble is that the elected representatives who seek to adorn the various seats of power are so busy politicking or safeguarding their own interests that they do not have time to think of the future of the State. They are so much pre-occupied with looking after their electorates and the interests of their family members or cronies that one wonders whether they have time to ponder over a vision for Mumbai in the 21st century. They do not even have an integrated vision of what should be done if money is available. They are trying to retain power and live from moment to moment and are totally unconcerned about the future generations of Mumbaikars or for that matter, of the entire State. The opposition parties on their part indulge in opposition for opposition's sake and are not ready to cooperate with the government of the day on larger issues of State's welfare by planning its expenditure, however meagre, on cultural issues for the next decade or so. They do not unite in the interest of the State and evolve a consensus on a common minimum agenda for the State or any of its cities, whatever the urgency. How could a comprehensive cultural policy be formulated if there is no consensus on basic issues? How can one drive home the need for formulating a comprehensive cultural policy in the interests of the citizens of tomorrow? In the absence of such an integrated visionary approach, every minister, every secretary of government department decides policy according to his whim, tries to implement it against all odds and opposition. But before the results of his new policy are visible, there is either a transfer of power and the minister is changed or the secretary transferred, leaving the supporters and implementers of the policy in lurch. Then a fresh start all over again: new minister or new secretary and new policy of the department! A classic case of this type of confusion is the policies of successive education ministers and the education secretaries on the teaching of English. One just has to count the number of times the decision of when to start teaching English, from what level of schooling, is reversed, to see how the government falters, hesitates, implements and withdraws its policies. Why not have the comprehensive views of experts and implement them with a resolve that the policy could be reversed only if 2/3rd members in the House allow it to be changed. Granted that no decision should be sacrosanct and the system should be flexible enough to accommodate new dictates of the market. Yet some way of stopping ministers from going berserk or wayward has to be evolved.

Here are some thoughts on comprehensive and integrated cultural policy:

The Language & Literature Policy

Nearly fifty years after the Maharashtra State celebrated its creation with fanfare, it has not been able to decide its language policy, particularly about English and also other languages such as Gujarati. It has not found ways and means of strengthening the study and teaching of Marathi which is the official language of the State. Obviously, the multi-language nature of Mumbai has posed a hurdle. Marathi is the State language, Hindi is the official national language and English is the World language. The study of these cannot be avoided. If an option is to be given to non-Marathi citizens, their mother tongues also will have to be on the list of preferences. Thus a four-language formula could have been the solution in Mumbai. But it is considered too much of a burden on a child to learn four languages simultaneously. Naturally teaching English suffers with the connivance of the government. In these days of globalisation can we afford to neglect the study of English? Does teaching English mean neglecting the mother-tongues of students? Vacillation in the policy for the study of languages has affected many generations of students in Maharashtra. Successive and quick changes in government's language policy have resulted in total apathy for the study of language and literature in the State. One minister feels one way while the other who succeeds him in his chair has exactly the opposite view of the situation. It is true that there are too many socio-cultural issues involved in teaching or not teaching English from the first standard in schools, but should we not decide once and for all the language policy of the State? Why should this be left to individual ministers or secretaries? There obviously is no alternative to Marathi which is the mother tongue of the local majority and also the State language. It is all right to say that Marathi should be the medium of instruction in schools, that it should be the language of government offices and in lower law courts. Impassioned public speeches are made in support of the greater use of Marathi, even resolutions are passed in its support in literary meets. But there are no takers for the argument that it is advisable to learn through the mother tongue. Pragmatic parents are seen sending their children in greater numbers to English medium schools from sheer necessity. They have realised that proficiency in English alone can prepare their wards to reach higher positions. The fact is that the Marathi language as it is taught in schools leaves much to be desired and graduates are coming out of the portals of colleges without proficiency in either language. The competitive market is vociferously demanding proficiency in English. It is hardly noticed by the political leaders that Marathi-speaking people are getting insular. They are cut off from the rest of the world, leave aside savouring the literary gems of the world language. The doors of world knowledge are thus closed to them. Marathi youth despite being good in other subjects are seen developing a sense of inferiority that is detrimental to their growth. Outsiders come and pocket good jobs which require working knowledge of English. When will our rulers realise that conflict is not between English and Marathi, that it is the result of apathy for the study of language and literature in general? Today's Marathi speaking generation is proficient in neither language, neither its own nor English. Despite tall talk and much display precious little is done by the Government to improve the teaching and learning of Marathi. The standard has deteriorated over the years.

The Government has not shown any will to change the situation. Why do our ministers speak in Marathi-English when foreign dignitaries visit them? Could they not speak in Marathi even if they do know a smattering of English? By doing this they will set examples before others, increase employment by making positions for interpreters and also show their pride in their mother tongue. Moreover if 'Hindi officers' could be appointed at All India Radio, Doordarshan and banks and government offices, why cannot 'Marathi officers' be appointed in cosmopolitan cities like Mumbai? The surprising part is that Marathi words and terms used in the official correspondence are difficult to understand for ordinary persons not introduced to the rich Sanskrit vocabulary. Moreover, since presently three sets of Marathi grammar rules are in vogue at the same time simultaneously, Marathi grammar has become chaotic and confusing. Moreover there was a movement to discard the standard Marathi on the ground that it is the language of a minority, the 'Brahmins of Pune'. The logic was that a minority cannot decide the 'standards'. But the Marathi spoken and written by the majority also has not been considered as 'standard'. Therefore Marathi is without a 'standard language' presently. First and foremost, the historical fact is that the tenets of Marathi grammar were standardised by the British lexicographers who were officials of the Education Department! If one 'standard language' is challenged and discarded, should not another standard replace it? A language that does not have a 'standard' variety is bound to increase confusion in the minds of its users. There is, therefore, the urgent need to have a clear cut language policy. The need is felt all the more as there are today a variety of computer programmes available for the Devnagari script. Should the Government not come forward to standardise the use of a Devnagari programme?

The Books & Public Libraries Policy

Following the UNESCO directive that there cannot be a tax on knowledge, it was clear that there cannot be any tax levied on books including octroi which is a Municipal jurisdiction. But the Thane Municipal Corporation levied octroi on books, as did the Kolhapur Municipal Corporation. Taxing books was considered a source of revenue, however meagre. When this was brought to the notice of the then Chief Minister Vilasrao Deshmukh, he promptly "abolished" the octroi on books. But the bureaucracy, not too happy with the Chief Minister's ruling issued a Government Resolution which stated "No tax of any kind on *essential* books." (Emphasis mine) This created more confusion as the term 'essential books' can mean different things to different people. To some, only religious books are essential, while to some children's books are essential. To some others only text-books are essential, to some, serious books on Western philosophy are not at all essential. It again required more appeals and representations before a corrigendum to the earlier Government Resolution regarding the octroi on books could be issued to the effect "No tax of any kind on any book in any language and on any subject."

Should a country of this size and with so many languages not have a uniform National Policy for

Books? An attempt was made, I believe, when Rajiv Gandhi was the Prime Minister. What happened to the National Book Policy is anybody's guess. The fact is that there appears to be a total absence of any official policy towards buying and selling of rare and antiquarian books. The State Government is oblivious to the fact that there ought to be a State policy towards collections, official or private, of rare and antiquarian books. Maharashtra was known for its network of public libraries. We have in the city and the State some really old libraries stocking extremely rare material. Any society would be proud to possess such valuable books. In fact, the collection of antique books, pieces of art and artefacts also is an indication of the progress of the society. In cities of advanced countries a lot of money is spent by the governments and government-encouraged industrial conglomerates, on libraries, museums and heritage buildings. But in our case antique books are fast depleting from Maharashtra. They are dwindling for want of extra funds or the expertise to preserve and conserve them. Libraries that have celebrated centenaries or post-centennial silver or golden jubilees are over a hundred in Maharashtra. There were in Mumbai a number of antiquarian book dealers. Today antiquarian book-dealing in Mumbai has almost become the reserve of a few individuals. Those antiquarian book-sellers who are somehow managing the show do so on what could at best be called second hand books. Old colleges such as the government-owned Elphinstone College and the Free Church Society of Scotland which runs the Wilson College have discarded many of their antique books. I can understand the predicament of their Principals and their Librarians for they have to create room for new books, but I cannot forgive them for their method of discarding. The State Government should have thought of setting up a Depository of Discarded Antique and Rare Books which, by law, should have been made to supervise any sale of such books. It would have been quite a logical step for a progressive State like Maharashtra. But in the absence of any such restrictions on machinery, antique and rare books found their way out of the country and none in the enlightened land of Maharashtra ever objected. That speaks for the attitude of the State Government and the concern of the citizens over squandering public wealth or heritage, whatever one calls it. The situation is so precarious that in the near future a researcher who would want to do research on any subject related to the erstwhile Bombay Presidency, would have to visit any of the following seven countries that are collecting books on the Indian themes at regular intervals: the U.K., U.S.A. France, Germany, Japan, Italy and Australia. Even if an individual buyer or an institutional representative wants to buy the books in the antique market, he is deterred by the prohibitive prices. But the same amounts, converted into sterling pounds or dollars, become attractive enough for buying those books. A foreign scholar can always take such 'gems' home, and sell them to interested academic libraries to subsidise his visit to India. He could do so lawfully, as there is no law that can prevent anybody from taking away antique and rare books out of the country. The archaic law prevents one from taking away manuscripts which are over 150 years old. In fact, the collections of antique and rare books in a country are an indication of its cultural richness; in the preservation and display of these for the benefit of scholars and laymen, is seen as progressive urges of the State Government. It is obvious that the present day government does not think so. As a result, antique book shops in Mumbai have dwindled over the years, for want of sufficient supply of books. Public and institutional libraries no longer possess good collections of antiquarian books which are either sold or given away to rag-pickers. There are no books for sale. Even then, personal collections made by great-grandfathers or grandfathers come out in the market. Once that stock depletes, even if you have the money and will to buy antique books, you may not get the books you want. Gujarat offers a typical example. At one point the region had over three hundred antiquarian bookshops commensurate with as many princely states. Each princely state chief took pride in patronising writers and poets by buying multiple copies of books. After the accession of these princely states these books in excellent condition found their way into these book shops. However, once those books were sold and were out of circulation, the book sellers in Gujarat had no other option but to switch over to the stationery trade. Only researchers of the 19th century western India know how difficult it is to procure books of the period. As a result, researches on western India lack comprehensiveness. Those who write in English rarely consult books in Marathi and Gujarati and those who write in Marathi and Gujarati cannot afford the English language books, as they are expensive due to the demand by foreign scholars. Some kind of a sectarian research is in the offing. Such a situation would have been avoided if the State governments had stepped in time to stop the drain of antiquarian and rare books out of the country. It is already late now, though the situation is not altogether beyond control. Disaster management is not only required to fight natural calamities, but also man-made problems.

Successive regimes in Maharashtra thought it more convenient to give away awards, where many a time mediocrity is awarded along with exceptionally creative. About a hundred and odd 'top' books are awarded by the government every year, whereas every year nearly thousand and odd new books are published in Marathi. Does one in every ten of the books really merit an award? The print order of a new book in Marathi for so many years has remained the same, a thousand copies despite new colleges and higher educational institutions multiplying and the literacy percentage growing every year. These days sometimes an edition of a new Marathi book consists of a meagre five hundred copies, that in State with a hundred million people. In Mumbai today literary awards for 'significant' literary works could be had for the asking, yet there is no major award for intellectual pursuits. Does it speak well of a progressive government if the writers and artistes can have awards on application? Awards for excellence in any field are an honour and an honour must come honourably and with due regard and respect. If the government wants its writers and artists to send in applications for being considered for any award, other literary and other institutions too are seen following suit, and would want them to apply and that too with two copies of the publication. Sending applications or lobbying for honours has become more and more open and at times unabashed. Would a writer who by definition is supposed to be self-respecting stoop low to lobby for any award? Or even send in an 'entry' which is yet another form of application? This is a two-way process. Writers, on their part, are not ready to be self-censors; they are not willing to evaluate their works on their own; publishers do not concede that a good writer can produce a bad work. They are interested in selling even the bad work of a successful writer. Common readers may not be able to distinguish between a good and bad book. They believe that all is well with the literary world and read what is easily available.

The Book Policy should have been innovative enough to encourage a literary culture rather than simply buying a certain number of copies under various schemes and then distributing them to public libraries. If the complaints of book-sellers are any indication, buying books centrally by the government has generated corruption of all kinds, and the government by now has become insensitive to criticism and manages to shield corrupt officials, perhaps even considers them more helpful than the non-corrupt. Buying of books published is not at all the job of the government. It should promote love of books in society. Why has some innovative minister or a learned bureaucrat not thought about a legal provision of having a book-shop at a distance of every kilometre?

Heritage and Museums Policy

The pathetic condition of museums shows up the government's poverty on fronts including that of ideas. First of all the government as well as the people at large do not have any idea of the impact museums have on young minds. Even if they have they do not want to spend money on informal ways of learning history. There are not many museums in the State, for their setting up is not encouraged. Those that are there in the cities are worth closing down, barring exceptions and if they are not closed they will close of themselves in the near future as they are already in deplorable conditions. We have refused to learn from other progressive countries how much money and effort goes in creating museums to preserve the inherited legacy, how much they spend on displaying their histories for the benefit of the future generations as well as foreign visitors. The reason that is every time brought forward is paucity of funds. Anybody could be silenced by the arguments that, with so many mouths to feed, bodies to clothe, and shelters to build, will it be proper to spend money on displaying our histories? But the reality is that it is not just paucity of funds, it is the lack of will to bring about a change. We have forgotten the old adage that 'a will will find a way'.

The Maharashtra State Archives, by far the richest one in the country, lies in neglect. Historical documents in its possession are crumbling to pieces, waiting for modern techniques of preservation and restoration. The Government cannot decide whether the building that houses it is actually meant for college or for the State Archives. The plan is sanctioned for a huge new building for keeping the archival records at a suburb, but no more progress is seen in that direction.

Fine Arts and Performing Arts Policy

There is a school of thought that considers that it is in the artistic records of a nation, much more than in the records of wars and dynastic changes, that the nation's true history is to be found. Paintings and sculptures, drama performances and music concerts are the expressions of the soul of country as they spring directly from great affirmations of spiritual consciousness. The universality and antiquity of art-expressions bear testimony as vital and essential parts of a nation's life. Presently however there is an estrangement between arts and life, between the principles that operate in the world of imagination and the world of social organisation and personal conduct. Signs of the lack of an awakened artistic consciousness are seen in the masses misguided to engage in corpulent and gaudy tastes in personal and social life. Indulging in the baser things of life arising out of ignorance keeps them away from the higher pleasures and upliftment fostered by beauty and vision that ennobling art experience promotes. "You cannot cut a people off from the art-expression which comes nearest to its own essential nature without loss to both the people and the art-expression," asserted James H. Cousins in an essay: 'The Arts and the Nation-Building' and emphasised, "A nation without art is blind and dumb. An art without nationality only awaits its transport to the burning ghat; and so, in any consideration of the arts as applied to national life, it is necessary to be clear that the arts that are sought to be applied in nation building are themselves national, national in expressing the national environment, the national temperament and the national direction."(*The Renaissance in India*, 1918, p. 29)

In a democracy, just as it is the responsibility of the State to encourage the arts by patronising them, it is also expected that the State educates and enlightens the public by developing the comprehension of artistic works by adopting various methods. But of late, the government's role has remained limited to awarding the artists chosen in a haphazard manner. The government feels it sufficient to award artists, give grants for their activities, and other mundane benefits. The artists too have no complaints.

★★★

A university or college teacher today does not enjoy the same social status and position of respectability in Mumbai as he or she did a few decades ago. He too like the newspaper editor has suffered in image. The writer or artist has ceased to have any impact on society. The state government should, in fact worry about the society whose new icons are only from Bollywood or from money-spinning sports like cricket. The Bollywoodisation of society is indicative of its de-intellectualisation. Symptoms of a de-intellectualised society are visible in almost all aspects of the Metropolis, and the unfortunate part of it is that neither the government nor those who are in the so called intellectual field seem to be concerned. In fact, rather than putting a stop to it or reversing the trend they seem hastening the process of de-intellectualisation. The Government of Maharashtra should have taken the lead long ago and should have asked some autonomous body to formulate a comprehensive cultural policy. It should have brought representatives from all walks of social life, cutting across political party lines, and tried its hand at a common minimum programme for an overall development of the city of Mumbai to make it comparable with any of the progressive cities of the world in thought and action. Merely spending millions of rupees on its makeover will not suffice. Town planners can take care of that. What could be done to bring it back to its position of intellectual leadership is an equally important issue. The city can be proud again if its intellectual leadership is restored and there does not appear to be a short cut to this process.

The authorities, somehow, pretend to believe that all is well with academic, literary and the art world. If the number of awards distributed every year is any indication the picture may appear quite healthy and ideal. However, it is not so. The picture is misleading. Just to take an example of the literary world, a prolific writer today becomes an eminent writer. A talkative writer is put in the class of quality writers and a shy, introvert writer is totally ignored even if he has extraordinary literary merit, even honours elude him.

He finds himself difficult to sell, to even get his books published. A self-advertiser occupies the front rank in a society which is greatly enamoured of adjectival prefixes, for in such a society only one rule prevails: nothing succeeds like excess. A Marathi newspaper carried a column for more than two years about the reading habits of prominent citizens. I kept a watchful eye on that column appearing weekly and was surprised to find that most of them either read popular fictional works or professional or religious literature, but hardly anyone ever read a serious literary or discursive, polemical work or a philosophical treatise or what could be called the mature literature.

It has been a common experience that government awards are generally rewards. They are in reality compensations for the help rendered to the powers that be in the retention of power. They are the prizes for maintaining friendship with the high and mighty in the government. The awards could be successful or unsuccessful attempts to buy silence from those who could be potential or current trouble-makers. In the recent past too awards were 'used' as instruments to please friends and silence detractors. But at least care was taken to include the names of some of deserving candidates. In the list of awardees these days, persons deserving government awards are found in the miniscule minority. The government has become so insensitive to criticism that its ministers and political leaders including thc shameless persons from the liberal professions who lobby for these awards, recommend friends and benefactors. Rarely does a person get an award without lobbying. Many an artist, thinker or writer has gone unnoticed. Moreover, there are so many awards every year that it is difficult to keep track of them. The number of awards is inversely proportional to the quality of awardees who do not feel it embarrassing to 'apply' or 'defray administrative cost'. In such a situation poor organisations expect the awardees to bear with them and 'cooperate'. The awards too are insignificant to preserve or gloat over. A small memento is sufficient to please a writer, a cultural 'leader' or an editor. It is to be accepted as a token of appreciation from the organisations. A time has come to make it obligatory to register the awards as there are instances when an award given to a friend is the first and the last time. However while naming the award in honour of some great son of the soil, no monetary provision is made and the closure follows. The registration of the award, say with the charity commissioner means, that an award once started should be run at least for ten years. The second condition should be that no organisation using the word Maharashtra in the name of the award be allowed to do so, for example, Maharashtra Ratna or Maharashtra Vaibhav or Maharashtra Gaurav, using the word 'Maharashtra' should be the prerogative only of the State Government.

This kind of a situation does not speak well for a

State that prides in calling itself *Maha-rashtra* (=great nation) and expects Mumbai, the Metropolis or Megapolis as it is proudly called, to boost our confidence to lead the other cities in making India a super power within a couple of decades.

Mumbai is evidently on the threshold of a new and prosperous era. International economists and town-planners who have understood its strategic importance—of being equidistant to both the worlds, Western and Eastern—are already predicting a greater international role for it that will bring unforeseen prosperity in the next hundred years. Even at present the middle class that is growing at a great speed in Mumbai is feeling that financially it never had it so good. However, the disparity is also growing at an equal speed. New tensions in the society are created by the widened and still widening gap between the 'haves' and the 'have-nots'. The signs of changing times are seen in the changing skylines of many areas in the city and also by ever increasing number of malls and Big Bazaars. The citizens have become aware of the city's urgent needs that require immediate attention. There is a growing pressure on the civic authorities to find short-term and long-term solutions to the city's long standing and new problems. The municipal government and the State Government can no longer postpone addressing the issues. With the increasing presence of international financial institutions, further commercial success awaits the city. This 'commercial capital of India' has consolidated its economic strength, but has not strengthened its wisdom, nor has it scaled greater intellectual heights. This may not work. The lop-sided economic growth will not regain for the city its intellectual, cultural and socio-political leadership. For that, all-sided growth is the only remedy.

Remarks made by Justice Ranade at the turn of the previous century, on the lop-sided development of society are pertinent even today. He had said:

> "You cannot have a good social system when you find yourself low in the scale of political rights, nor can you be fit to exercise political rights and privileges unless your social system is based on reason and justice. You cannot have a good economical system when your social arrangements are imperfect. If your religious ideals are low and grovelling, you cannot succeed in social, economic and political spheres. This interdependence is not an accident but is the law of our nature. Like the members of our body you cannot have strength in hands and feet, if your internal organs are in disorder. What is applied to the human body holds good of the collective humanity we call society or State." (*Religious and Social Reforms*, 1902, p. xxxxix)

There was an interesting controversy in the 19th century: whether the Oriental brain has worn out through overuse? Has the ancient civilisation got exhausted and run out of steam? These were difficult questions to answer. But for sure, we have moved away from our commitment to intellect, oblivious of the fact that it is not sufficient to produce technology savvy graduates, equipped with fair amounts of job knowledge. The ultimate aim of higher learning is to create a proper intellectual climate in society which will help create superior minds, and the rest will follow. For a modern university improving the quality of social life by creating a humane, just and fair world is an important but too modest an aim. What we require to do is to venture into the realm of ideas in search of truth. A beginning can be made by inspiring the younger generations, literally goading them into debates and discussions while we lead them to various kinds of research laboratories. Rejoicing in the success of scientists like ECG alias George Sudarshan and Hargobind Khorana or of Amartya Sen is akin to self-deception. Most of their work was conducted in foreign lands. Even Dr. Homi Bhabha who is credited with the Bhabha-Heitler Cascade Theory did his work mostly in Cambridge. We have not produced in the post-Independence period the likes of Satyendranath Bose with his "Bose's statistics" (1924), Meghnath Saha with his "Ionisation formula" (1926), C.V. Raman with his "Raman effect (1928)" or Chandrasekhar with his "Chandrasekhar Limit" (1930-32) who worked on Indian soil. And the sad part is that not even one of these is from Mumbai. Mumbai no doubt produced a few scientists and social scientists of recognisable calibre but few could reach world class stature, and the reason for this is that the climate around them was not intellectual enough. Mumbai has in the past few decades not produced a single great social scientist leave aside a thinker. The situation is not any different in the other fields.

The decline of intellectualism is obviously seen in that even sixty years after independence, no political party worth the name feels the dire need of think-tanks. Mrs. Indira Gandhi had her Kitchen Cabinet of Delhi intellectuals for a short while. One of the Prime Ministers tried to endear himself to the people of the country by establishing himself as a non-intellectual and projecting his own image as a 'humble farmer'. From then on there was as if a competition among farmer-politicians of the country to exhibit their 'humbler than thou' attitude. None, however, questioned oneself as to whether a humble farmer can ever become Prime Minister of India. It is all too obvious that politicians look upon 'thinking men' as their enemies. The 'thinking men' too find it more profitable to be apologists rather than critics of the establishment. But perhaps this was so in all ages. Those in authority are too quick to stall any protest of intellectuals by the power of patronage conferring awards, subsidising their activities or creating positions in various boards or committees.

I could be blamed for passing a harsh judgement too soon and generalising. But does not any generalisation leave scope for exceptions? There no doubt are honourable exceptions and it is they who in reality run the show. But I have used harsh language with the intention of taking this issue out of its larger context, magnifying it and putting it under the scanner with the hope of making it available to be debatable in wider circles, as this is the dire need of the hour.

The decline of intellectualism has affected all the liberal professions-—teachers, writers, lawyers, journalists—in fact all those wordsmiths whose professions require them to deal with words for informing and educating society at large. Their power of ideas makes society at large *think*. For without thinking and theorising, society starts indulging in epicurean pleasures and forgets the higher aims of life. What wonder then if Mumbai society today largely *imitates* instead of *innovating*, whereas the aim of every progressive society should be to think, theorise and innovate, rather than imitate, copy and fall together. I have chosen to discuss at some length four of these major fields—the literary field, academia, media and culture—that have brought us to this intellectual bankruptcy and led our society at large to a de-intellectualised state.

It must be remembered that a society whose intellectuals do not perform their social function of speaking the truth, of remaining disinterested, of challenging the authority whenever occasions demand will be increasingly dwarfed, even if the list of the 'government approved' scholars and intellectuals becomes longer and longer every year: A society whose politicians and leaders do not hesitate to publicly deride its intellectuals is bound to face a crisis of standards. A society whose members are in search of the proverbial golden fleece, and shun anything that has a stamp of intellectual activity, a society that does not respect its intellectuals, a society whose intellectuals are too timid to displease the authority, is bound to generate an ethos of anti-intellectualism. A society that does not consider ideas as power goes down in all walks of life.

That many societies elsewhere have gone through such a phase is evident from John Stuart Mill remarks. He said:

> "The worth of a State, in the long run, is the worth of the individuals composing it; and a State which postpones the interests of *their* mental expansion amd elevation, to a little more administrative skill, or of that semblance of it which practice gives, in the details of business; a State which dwarfs its men, in order that they may be docile instruments in its hands even for beneficial purposes—will find that with small men no great thing can really be accomplished..." (*On Liberty*, 1859, p. 267)

If those societies, recovered from such a state, why can't we do so?

Thomas S. Kuhn in his celebrated book: *The Structure of Scientific Revolutions* recommends a total change in paradigms, the alteration of the framework of inquiry, raising new sets of questions and seeking replies to them. Without such changes there cannot be advance in knowledge. Knowledge, all said and done, is at the root of all intellectual progress. Unless the intellectuals of the society come forward to execute their social responsibility, society and its culture will deteriorate speedily. If this happens it will be a sad day for Mumbai and Mumbaikars. But if they do come forward, it will be a new beginning for realising the dream of better tomorrow.

Bibliography

Adler, Mortimer J.: *A Second Look in the Rearview Mirror—Further Autobiographical Reflections of a Philosopher at Large*, MacMillan Publishing Company, New York, 1992.

Amrik Singh (ed.): *The Craft of Teaching*, Konark Publishers, 1995.

Beteille, Andre: *Ideologies and Intellectuals*, Oxford University Press, Delhi, 1980.

Berlin, Isaiah: *The Power of Ideas*, ed. by Henry Hardy, Princeton University Press, Princeton and Oxford, 1995.

Bloch Marc: *The Historian's Craft*, Manchester University Press, Manchester, 1954.

Bloom, Allan: *Closing of the American Mind*, Simon and Schuster, New York, 1987.

Caudwell, Christopher: *Studies in a Dying Culture*, John Lane The Bodley Head, Lodon,1938, Reprinted 1947.

Chakladar, H.C.: *Social Life in Ancient India*, Sisir Gupta (India) Ltd, Calcutta, 2nd Rev. ed.,1954.

Chaudhuri, Nirad C.: *The Intellectual in India*, Vir Publishing House, New Delhi, 1967.

Choudhary, Kameshwar: *Intellectuals and Society—A Study of Teachers in India*, Popular Prakshan, Mumbai, 2004.

Cotton, J.S.: *Mountstuart Elphinstone* (Rulers of India Series), Oxford University Press, 1892.

Cousins, Jmes H.: *The Renaissance in India*, Ganesh & Co., Madras, 1918.

Crig, Gordon A.: *The Germans*, New American Library, New York, 1982.

Croce Benedetto: *History—Its Theory and Practice*, New York, 1921.

Dobbin, Christine: *Urban Leadership in Western India—Politics and Communities in Bombay City, 1840-1885*; Oxford University Press, London, 1972.

Durant Will: *Pleasures of Philosophy*, Simon and Schuster, New York, 1953.

Edwardes, S.M.: *The Gazetteer of Bombay City and Island*, Vol. I-III, 1909.

Eliot, T.S.: *The Writer and His Community*: The Twenty-first W.P. Ker Memorial Lecture, University of Glasgow, 15 October, 1965, Jakson, J & Company, Glasgow, 1968.

Fontana Dictionary of Modern Thought, ed. by Allan Bullock and others, 1977.

Fowles, John: *Wormholes—Essays and Occasional Writings*, ed. and introd. by Jan Relf, Vintage, (1998), 1999 imprint.

Gramsci, Antonio: *Selections from Prison Notebooks*, ed. and trans. by Quintin Hoare and Geoffrey Nowell Smith, Lawrence and Wishart, London, 1971, 1991 printing.

Gross, John: *The Rise and Fall of the Man of Letters—Aspects of English Literary Life Since 1800*, Weidenfeld and Nicolson, London, 1969.

Hardy, G.H.: *A Mathematician's Apology*, with a Foreword by C.P. Snow, Cambridge University Press, First Published 1940, Canto edition, 1992, Reprint 1993.

Herzog, Don: *Poisoning the Minds of the Lower Orders*, Princeton University Press, Princeton, New Jersey, First Paperback Printing, 2000.

Himmelfarb, Gertrude: *The Roads to Modernity—The British, French, and American Enlightenments,* Vintage Books, New York, 2005.

Janeway, Michael: *Republic of Denial—Press, Politics and Public Life,* Yale University Press, New Haven & London, 1999.

Jha, Akhileshwar: *Intellectuals at the Crossroads,* Vikas Publishing, New Drlhi, 1977.

Kagarlitsky, Boris: *Thinking Reed—Intellectuals and the Soviet State from 1917 to the Present,* Trans. by Brian Pearce, Verso, London 1988, 1989 paperback ed.

Kalam, A. P. J. Abdul, with Rajan Y. S.: *India 2020—A Vision for the New Millenium,* Viking, New Delhi, 1998.

Kerr, Clark: *The Uses of the University* (The Godkin Lectures), Harvard University Press, Massechusetts, 1963.

Kunh, Thomas S.: *The Structure of Scientific Revolutions,* Second ed., enlarged, 1986.

Lilla, Mark: *The Reckless Mind—Intellectuals and Politics,* Review Books, New York, 2001.

Levine, Lawrence W: *The Opening of the American Mind – Canons. Culture, and History,* Beacon, 1997.

Mandlik, Vishvanath Narayan: *Transactions of the Literary Society of Bombay,* The Society, Bombay, Vols. I-III, 1877.

Mankar, G.A.: *A Sketch of the Life and Works of the late Mr. Justice M.G. Ranade,* Caxton Printing Works, Bombay, Vol. I & II, 1902.

Masselos, Jim: *Towards Nationalism,* Popular Prakashan, Bombay, 1974.

Mill, John Stuart (ed. by David Spitz) : *On Liberty,* W. Norton & Co, New York, 1975.

Mote, Frederick W.: *Intellectual Foundations of China*, Alfred A. Knopf, New York, 1971.

Morle, John: *On Compromise*, 1921, 1933 ed.

Narby, Jeremy: *Intelligence in Nature—An Inquiry into Knowledge*, Penguin, New York, 2005.

Nisbett, Richard E.: *The Geography of Thought—How Asians and Westerners Think Differently...and Why*, Free Press, New York, 2003.

Orwell, George (ed. & introd. By John Carey): *Essays*, Everyman Library, 1998.

Ostrower, Francie: *Why the Wealthy Give—The Culture of Elite Philanthropy*, Princeton University Press, Princeton, New Jersey, 1995.

Phatak, N. R.: *Presidential address of the Akhil Bharatiya Marathi Sahitya Sammelan*, Hyderabad, 1947. (Marathi)

Pitale, Balkrishna Nilaji (comp. & ed.): *The Speeches and Addresses of Sir H.E.B. Frere*, Pitale, Bombay, 1870.

Pope, Alexander (ed. by Robert Carruthers): *The Poetical Works of Alexander Pope*, Vols. I-IV, Nathaniel Cooke, London, 1853.

Priyalkar, Anant Kakba: *Doktar Bhau Daji—Vyakti, Kaal va Kartrutva*, Marathi Sahitya Sangh, Mumbai, 1971 (Marathi).

Ranade, M.G.: *Religious and Social Reforms—A Collection of Essays and Speeches*, collected and compiled by M.B. Kolasker, Gopal Norayan & Co., Bombay, 1902.

Said, Edward: *Representations of an Intellectual,* The 1993 Reith Lectures, Vintage Books, 1994.

Snow, C.P.: *The Two Cultures*, with Intro. By Stefan Collini, Cambridge University Press, Canto ed. 1993.

Tikekar, Aroon: *The Cloister's Pale—A Biography of the University of Mumbai*, Popular Prakashan, Bombay, 2006.

Tikekar, Aroon: *Dr. George Buist of the Bombay Times*, in N.K. Wagle (ed.): *Writers, Editors and Reformers of Maharashtra, 1830–1930*, Manohar, New Delhi, 1999.

Tikekar, Aroon: *Ranade—The Renaissance Man*, Shri Vidya Prakashan, Pune, 2000.

Tivarekar, Ganapatrao Krishna: *Index of the Transactions of the Literary Society of Bombay*, Vols.I-III and the *Journals of the Bombay Branch, Royal Asiatic Society*, Vols I- XVII, With a Historical Sketch of the Society, The Society, Bombay, 1886.

Index